AF303971
Marx Hardy Defoe Abbott Melville Machiavelli Montaigne Haggard Chesterton Cooper Emerson Joyce Austen Hugo Eliot Grimm
Stoker Carroll Christie Maupassant Byron Molière Schiller
Wilde Garnett Einstein Fitzgerald Engels Smith Kafka Hall
Goethe Hawthorne Dostoyevsky Willis
Cotton Kipling Doyle
Baum Henry Nietzsche Balzac Crane
Leslie Dumas Flaubert Turgenev Verne
Stockton Vatsyayana Vinci
Burroughs Whitman Gogol Busch
Curtis Tocqueville
Homer Widger Tolstoy Twain Scott Plato Harte
Darwin Thoreau
Potter Freud Zola Lawrence Dickens Hesse
Kant Jowett Stevenson Burton
Andersen Cervantes
London Descartes Voltaire Cooke
Poe Aristotle Wells
Hale James Hastings
Bunner Shakespeare Chambers Irving
Richter da Shaw Wodehouse Benedict Alcott
Doré Dante Chekhov Pushkin
Swift Newton

tredition was established in 2006 by Sandra Latusseck and Soenke Schulz. Based in Hamburg, Germany, tredition offers publishing solutions to authors and publishing houses, combined with world-wide distribution of printed and digital book content. tredition is uniquely positioned to enable authors and publishing houses to create books on their own terms and without conventional manufacturing risks.

For more information please visit: www.tredition.com

TREDITION CLASSICS

This book is part of the TREDITION CLASSICS series. The creators of this series are united by passion for literature and driven by the intention of making all public domain books available in printed format again - worldwide. Most TREDITION CLASSICS titles have been out of print and off the bookstore shelves for decades. At tredition we believe that a great book never goes out of style and that its value is eternal. Several mostly non-profit literature projects provide content to tredition. To support their good work, tredition donates a portion of the proceeds from each sold copy. As a reader of a TREDITION CLASSICS book, you support our mission to save many of the amazing works of world literature from oblivion. See all available books at www.tredition.com.

Project Gutenberg

The content for this book has been graciously provided by Project Gutenberg. Project Gutenberg is a non-profit organization founded by Michael Hart in 1971 at the University of Illinois. The mission of Project Gutenberg is simple: To encourage the creation and distribution of eBooks. Project Gutenberg is the first and largest collection of public domain eBooks.

The Day of Sir John Macdonald A Chronicle of the First Prime Minister of the Dominion

Joseph, Sir Pope

Imprint

This book is part of TREDITION CLASSICS

Author: Joseph, Sir Pope
Cover design: Buchgut, Berlin – Germany

Publisher: tredition GmbH, Hamburg - Germany
ISBN: 978-3-8472-1722-0

www.tredition.com
www.tredition.de

Copyright:
The content of this book is sourced from the public domain.

The intention of the TREDITION CLASSICS series is to make world literature in the public domain available in printed format. Literary enthusiasts and organizations, such as Project Gutenberg, worldwide have scanned and digitally edited the original texts. tredition has subsequently formatted and redesigned the content into a modern reading layout. Therefore, we cannot guarantee the exact reproduction of the original format of a particular historic edition. Please also note that no modifications have been made to the spelling, therefore it may differ from the orthography used today.

**Sir John Macdonald crossing the Rockies over the newly con-
structed Canadian Pacific Railway, 1886.
From a colour drawing by C. W. Jefferys**

THE DAY OF
SIR JOHN MACDONALD

A Chronicle of the First Prime Minister
of the Dominion

BY

SIR JOSEPH POPE

K.C.M.G.

TORONTO
GLASGOW, BROOK & COMPANY
1915

{vii}

PREFATORY NOTE

Within a short time will be celebrated the centenary of the birth of the great statesman who, half a century ago, laid the foundations and, for almost twenty years, guided the destinies of the Dominion of Canada.

Nearly a like period has elapsed since the author's *Memoirs of Sir John Macdonald* was published. That work, appearing as it did little more than three years after his death, was necessarily subject to many limitations and restrictions. As a connected story it did not profess to come down later than the year 1873, nor has the time yet arrived for its continuation and completion on the same lines. That task is probably reserved for other and freer hands than mine. At the same time, it seems desirable that, as Sir John Macdonald's centenary approaches, there should be available, in convenient form, a short résumé of the salient features of his {viii} career, which, without going deeply and at length into all the public questions of his time, should present a familiar account of the man and his work as a whole, as well as, in a lesser degree, of those with whom he was intimately associated. It is with such object that this little book has been written.

JOSEPH POPE.
OTTAWA, 1914.

{ix}

{1}

CHAPTER I

YOUTH

John Alexander Macdonald, second son of Hugh Macdonald and Helen Shaw, was born in Glasgow on January 11, 1815. His father, originally from Sutherlandshire, removed in early life to Glasgow, where he formed a partnership with one M'Phail, and embarked in business as a cotton manufacturer. Subsequently he engaged in the manufacture of bandanas, and the style of the firm became 'H. Macdonald and Co.' The venture did not prove successful, and Macdonald resolved to try his fortunes in the New World. Accordingly, in the year 1820, he embarked for Canada in the good ship *Earl of Buckinghamshire*, and after a voyage long and irksome even for those days, landed at Quebec and journeyed overland to Kingston, then and for some years after the most considerable town in Upper Canada, boasting a population (exclusive of the military) of about 2500 souls.

{2}

At that time the whole population of what is now the province of Ontario did not exceed 120,000, clustered, for the most part, in settlements along the Bay of Quinté, Lake Ontario proper, and the vicinity of the Niagara and Detroit rivers. The interior of the province was covered with the primeval forest, which disappeared slowly, and only by dint of painful and unceasing toil. The early accounts of Kingston bear eloquent testimony to its primitive character. In 1815, according to a correspondent of the Kingston *Gazette*, the town possessed no footways worthy of the name, in consequence of which lack it was, during rainy weather, 'scarcely possible to move about without being in mud to the ankles.' No provision existed for lighting the streets 'in the dark of the moon'; a fire-engine was badly needed, and also the enforcement of a regulation prohibiting the piling of wood in public thoroughfares.

Communication with the outside world, in those early days, was slow, toilsome, and sometimes dangerous. The roads were, for the most part, Indian paths, somewhat improved in places, but utterly unsuited, particularly in spring and autumn, for the passage of heavily laden vehicles. In 1817 a weekly {3} stage began running from Kingston to York (Toronto), with a fare of eighteen dollars. The opening of an overland highway between Kingston and Montreal, which could be travelled on by horses, was hailed as a great boon. Prior to this the journey to Montreal had been generally made by water, in an enlarged and improved type of bateau known as a Durham boat, which had a speed of two to three miles an hour. The cost to the passenger was one cent and a half a mile, including board.

In the early twenties of the nineteenth century the infant province of Upper Canada found itself slowly recovering from the effects of the War of 1812-14. Major-General Sir Peregrine Maitland, the lieutenant-governor, together with the Executive and Legislative Councils, was largely under the influence of the 'Family Compact' of those days. The oligarchical and selfish rule of this coterie gave rise to much dissatisfaction among the people, whose discontent, assiduously fanned by agitators like Robert Gourlay, culminated in open rebellion in the succeeding decade.

Such was the condition of things prevailing at the time when the future prime minister arrived in the town with which he was destined {4} to be in close association for nearly three-quarters of a century.

**The Macdonald homestead at Adolphustown.
From a print in the John Ross Robertson Collection,
Toronto Public Library**

Hugh Macdonald, after a few years of unsatisfactory experience in Kingston, determined upon seeking fortune farther west. Accordingly he moved up the Bay of Quinté to the township of Adolphustown, which had been settled about forty years previously by a party of United Empire Loyalists under the command of one Captain Van Alstine. Here, at Hay Bay, Macdonald opened a shop. Subsequently he moved across the Bay of Quinté to a place in the county of Prince Edward, known then as the Stone Mills, and afterwards as Glenora, where he built a grist-mill. This undertaking, however, did not prosper, and in 1836 he returned to Kingston, where he obtained a post in the Commercial Bank. Shortly afterwards he fell into ill health, and in 1841 he died.

Few places in the wide Dominion of Canada possess greater charm than the lovely arm of Lake Ontario beside whose pleasant waters Sir John Macdonald spent the days of his early boyhood. The settlements had been founded by Loyalists who had left the United States rather than join in revolution. The lad lived in daily contact with men who had {5} given the strongest possible testimony of their loyalty, in relinquishing all that was dear to them rather than forswear allegiance to their king, and it is not surprising that he imbibed, in the morning of life, those principles of devotion to the crown and to British institutions which regulated every stage of his subsequent career. To the last he never forgot the Bay of Quinté, and whenever I passed through that charming locality in his company he would speak with enthusiasm of the days when he lived there. He would recall some event connected with each neighbourhood, until, between Glasgow and Kingston, Adolphustown, Hay Bay, and the Stone Mills, it was hard to tell what was his native place. I told him so one day, and he laughingly replied: 'That's just what the Grits say. The *Globe* has it that I am born in a new place every general election!'

When Hugh Macdonald moved from Hay Bay to the Stone Mills, his son John, then about ten years of age, returned to Kingston to pursue his studies. He attended the grammar school in that town until he reached the age of fifteen, when he began the world for himself. Five years at a grammar school was all the formal education Sir John {6} Macdonald ever enjoyed. To reflect upon the vast fund of knowledge of all kinds which he acquired in after years by his reading, his observation, and his experience, is to realize to the full the truth of the saying, that a man's education often begins with his leaving school. He always regretted the disadvantages of his early life. 'If I had had a university education,' I heard him say one day, 'I should probably have entered upon the path of literature and acquired distinction therein.' He did not add, as he might have done, that the successful government of millions of men, the strengthening of an empire, the creation of a great dominion, call for the possession and exercise of rarer qualities than are necessary to the achievement of literary fame.

In 1830 Macdonald, then fifteen years of age, entered upon the study of law in the office of George Mackenzie of Kingston, a close friend of his father, with whom also he lodged. In 1832 Mackenzie opened a branch office in the neighbouring town of Napanee, to which place Macdonald was occasionally sent to look after the business. In 1833, by an arrangement made between Mackenzie and L. P. Macpherson—a relative of the Macdonalds—young {7} Macdonald was sent to Picton, to take charge of Macpherson's law-office during his absence from Canada.

On being called to the bar in 1836, Macdonald opened an office in Kingston and began the practice of law on his own account. In the first year of his profession, there entered his office as student a lad destined to become, in Ontario, scarcely less eminent than himself. This was Oliver Mowat, the son of Macdonald's intimate personal and political friend, John Mowat of Kingston. Oliver Mowat studied law four years with Macdonald, leaving his office in 1840. About the same time another youth, likewise destined to achieve more than local celebrity as Sir Alexander Campbell, applied for admission to the office. Few circumstances in the political history of Canada have been more dwelt upon than this noteworthy association; few are more worthy of remark. A young man, barely twenty-one years of age, without any special advantages of birth or education, opens a law-office in Kingston, at that time a place of less than five thousand inhabitants. Two lads come to him to study law. The three work together for a few years. They afterwards go into politics. One drifts away {8} from the other two, who remain closely allied. After the lapse of twenty-five years the three meet again, at the Executive Council Board, members of the same Administration. Another twenty-five years roll by, and the principal is prime minister of Canada, while one of the students is lieutenant-governor of the great province of Ontario, the other his chief adviser, and all three are decorated by Her Majesty for distinguished services to the state.

The times were rough. In Macdonald's first case, which was at Picton, he and the opposing counsel became involved in an argument, which, waxing hotter and hotter, culminated in blows. They closed and fought in open court, to the scandal of the judge, who immediately instructed the crier to enforce order. This crier was an old man, personally much attached to Macdonald, in whom he took a lively interest. In pursuance of his duty, however, he was compelled to interfere. Moving towards the combatants, and circling round them, he shouted in stentorian tones, 'Order in the court, order in the court!' adding in a low, but intensely sympathetic voice as he passed near his protégé, 'Hit him, John!' I have heard Sir John Macdonald {9} say that, in many a parliamentary encounter of after years, he has seemed to hear, above the excitement of the occasion, the voice of the old crier whispering in his ear the words of encouragement, 'Hit him, John!'

In 1837 the rebellion broke out, and Macdonald hastened to give his services to the cause of law and order. 'I carried my musket in '37,' he was wont to say in after years. One day he gave me an account of a long march his company made, I forget from what place, but with Toronto as the objective point. 'The day was hot, my feet were blistered—I was but a weary boy—and I thought I should have dropped under the weight of the flint musket which galled my shoulder. But I managed to keep up with my companion, a grim old soldier, who seemed impervious to fatigue.'

In 1838 took place the notorious Von Shoultz affair, about which much misunderstanding exists. The facts are these. During the rebellion of 1837-38 a party of Americans crossed the border and captured a windmill near Prescott, which they held for eight days. They were finally dislodged, arrested, and tried by court-martial. The quartermaster of the insurgents was a man named Gold. He {10} was taken, as was also Von Shoultz, a Polish gentleman. Gold had a brother-in-law in Kingston, named Ford. Ford was anxious that some effort should be made to defend his relative. Leading lawyers refused the service. One morning Ford came to Macdonald's house before he was up. After much entreaty he persuaded Macdonald to undertake the defence. There could be practically no defence, however, and Von Shoultz, Gold, and nine others were condemned and hanged. Von Shoultz's career had been chequered. He was born in Cracow. His father, a major in a Cracow regiment, was killed in action while fighting for the cause of an independent Poland, and on the field of battle his son was selected by the corps to fill his father's place. He afterwards drifted about Europe until he reached Florence, where he taught music for a while. There he married an English girl, daughter of an Indian officer, General Mackenzie. Von Shoultz subsequently crossed to America, settled in Virginia, took out a patent for crystallizing salt, and acquired some property. The course of business took him to Salina, N.Y., not far from the Canadian boundary, where he heard of the rebellion going on in Canada. He not unnaturally {11} associated the cause of the rebels with that of his Polish brethren warring against oppression. He had been told that the Canadians were serfs, fighting for liberty. Fired with zeal for such a cause, he crossed the frontier with a company and was captured. He was only second in command, the nominal chief being a Yankee named Abbey, who tried to run away, and who, Von Shoultz declared to Macdonald, was a coward.

Von Shoultz left to Macdonald a hundred dollars in his will. 'I wish my executors to give Mr John A. Macdonald $100 for his kindness to me.' This was in the original draft, but Macdonald left it out when reading over the will for his signature. Von Shoultz observed the omission, and said, 'You have left that out.' Macdonald replied yes, that he would not take it. 'Well,' replied Von Shoultz, 'if it cannot be done one way, it can another.' So he wrote with his own hand a letter of instructions to his executors to pay this money over, but Macdonald refused to accept it.

It has been generally stated that it was the 'eloquent appeal' on behalf of this unfortunate man which established Macdonald's reputation at the bar, but this is quite a mistake. {12} Macdonald never made any speech in defence of Von Shoultz, for two very good reasons. First, the Pole pleaded guilty at the outset; and, secondly, the trial was by court-martial, on which occasions, in those days, counsel were not allowed to address the court on behalf of the prisoner.

This erroneous impression leads me to say that a good deal of misapprehension exists respecting the early manhood of Canada's first prime minister. He left school, as we have seen, at an age when many boys begin their studies. He did this in order that he might assist in supporting his parents and sisters, who, from causes which I have indicated, were in need of his help. The responsibility was no light one for a lad of fifteen. Life with him in those days was a struggle; and all the glamour with which writers seek to invest it, who begin their accounts by mysterious allusions to the mailed barons of his line, is quite out of place. His grandfather was a merchant in a Highland village. His father served his apprenticeship in his grandfather's shop, and he himself was compelled to begin the battle of life when a mere lad. Sir John Macdonald owed nothing to birth or fortune. He did not think little of either of them, but it is the {13} simple truth to say that he attained the eminent position which he afterwards occupied solely by his own exertions. He was proud of this fact, and those who thought to flatter him by asserting the contrary little knew the man. Nor is it true that he leaped at one bound into the first rank of the legal profession. On the contrary, I believe that his progress at the bar, although uniform and constant, was not extraordinarily rapid. He once told me that he was unfortunate, in the beginning of his career, with his criminal cases, several of his clients, of whom Von Shoultz was one, having been hanged. This piece of ill luck was so marked that somebody (I think it was William Henry Draper, afterwards chief justice) said to him, jokingly, one day, 'John A., we shall have to make you attorney-general, owing to your success in *securing* convictions!'

Age 27   1842

John A. Macdonald in 1842

Macdonald's mother was in many ways a remarkable woman. She had great energy and strength of will, and it was she, to use his own words, who 'kept the family together' during their first years in Canada. For her he ever cherished a tender regard, and her death, which occurred in 1862, was a great grief to him.

{14}

The selection of Kingston by Lord Sydenham in 1840 as the seat of government of the united provinces of Canada was a boon to the town. Real property advanced in price, some handsome buildings were erected, apart from those used as public offices, and a general improvement in the matter of pavements, drains, and other public utilities became manifest. Meanwhile, however, Toronto had far outstripped its sometime rival. In 1824 the population of Toronto (then York) had been less than 1700, while that of Kingston had been about 3000, yet in 1848 Toronto counted 23,500 inhabitants to Kingston's 8400. Still, Kingston jogged along very comfortably, and Macdonald added steadily to his reputation and practice. On September 1, 1843, he formed a partnership with his quondam student Alexander Campbell, who had just been admitted to the bar. It was not long before Macdonald became prominent as a citizen of Kingston. In March 1843 he was elected to the city council for what is now a portion of Frontenac and Cataraqui wards. But a higher destiny awaited him.

The rebellion which had broken out in Lower Canada and spread to the upper {15} province, while the future prime minister was quietly applying himself to business, had been suppressed. In Upper Canada, indeed, it had never assumed a serious character. Its leaders, or some of them at any rate, had received the reward of their transgressions. Lord Durham had come to Canada, charged with the arduous duty of ascertaining the cause of the grave disorders which afflicted the colony. He had executed his difficult task with rare skill, but had gone home broken-hearted to die, leaving behind him a report which will ever remain a monument no less to his powers of observation and analysis than to the clearness and vigour of his literary style.[1] The {16} union of Upper and Lower Canada, advocated by Lord Durham, had taken place. The seat of government had been fixed at Kingston, and the experiment of a united Canada had begun.

We have seen that Macdonald, at the outbreak of the rebellion, hastened to place his military services at the disposal of the crown. On the restoration of law and order we find his political sympathies ever on the side of what used to be called the governor's party. This does not mean that at any time of his career he was a member of, or in full sympathy with, the high Toryism of the 'Family Compact.' In those days he does not even seem to have classed himself as a Tory.[2] Like many moderate men in the province, Macdonald sided with this party because he hated sedition. The members of the 'Family {17} Compact' who stood by the governor were devotedly loyal to the crown and to monarchical institutions, while the violent language of some of the Radical party alienated many persons who, while they were not Tories, were even less disposed to become rebels.

The exacting demands of his Radical advisers upon the governor-general at this period occasionally passed all bounds. One of their grievances against Sir Charles Metcalfe was that he had ventured to appoint on his personal staff a Canadian gentleman bearing the distinguished name of deSalaberry, who happened to be distasteful to LaFontaine. In our day, of course, no minister could dream of interfering, even by way of suggestion, with a governor-general in the selection of his staff. In 1844, when the crisis came, and Metcalfe appealed to the people of Canada to sustain him, Macdonald sought election to the Assembly from Kingston. It was his 'firm belief,' he announced at the time, 'that the prosperity of Canada depends upon its permanent connection with the mother country'; and he was determined to 'resist to the utmost any attempt (from whatever quarter it may come) which may tend to {18} weaken that union.' He was elected by a large majority.

In the same year, the year in which Macdonald was first elected to parliament, another young Scotsman, likewise to attain great prominence in the country, made his *début* upon the Canadian stage. On March 5, 1844, the Toronto *Globe* began its long and successful career under the guidance of George Brown, an active and vigorous youth of twenty-five, who at once threw himself with great energy and conspicuous ability into the political contest that raged round the figure of the governor-general. Brown's qualities were such as to bring him to the front in any labour in which he might engage. Ere long he became one of the leaders of the Reform party, a position which he maintained down to the date of his untimely death at the hands of an assassin in 1880. Brown did not, however, enter parliament for some years after the period we are here considering.

The Conservative party issued from the general elections of 1844 with a bare majority in the House, which seldom exceeded six and sometimes sank to two or three. Early in that year the seat of government had been removed from Kingston to Montreal. The first {19} session of the new parliament—the parliament in which Macdonald had his first seat—was held in the old Legislative Building which occupied what was afterwards the site of St Anne's Market. In those days the residential quarter was in the neighbourhood of Dalhousie Square, the old Donegana Hotel on Notre Dame Street being the principal hostelry in the city. There it was that the party chiefs were wont to forgather. That Macdonald speedily attained a leading position in the councils of his party is apparent from the fact that he had not been two years and a half in parliament when the prime minister, the Hon. W. H. Draper, wrote him (March 4, 1847) requesting his presence in Montreal. Two months later Macdonald was offered and accepted a seat in the Cabinet.

Almost immediately after Macdonald's admission to the Cabinet, Draper retired to the bench. He was succeeded by Henry Sherwood, a scion of the 'Family Compact,' whose term of office was brief. The elections came on during the latter part of December, and, as was very generally expected,[3] the {20} Sherwood Administration went down to defeat. In Lower Canada the Government did not carry a single French-Canadian constituency, and in Upper Canada they failed of a majority, taking only twenty seats out of forty-two. In accordance with the more decorous practice of those days, the Ministry, instead of accepting their defeat at the hands of the press, met parliament like men, and awaited the vote of want of confidence from the people's representatives. This was not long in coming; whereupon they resigned, and the Reform leaders Baldwin and LaFontaine reigned in their stead.

The events of the next few years afford a striking example of the mutability of political life. Though this second Baldwin-LaFontaine Administration was elected to power by a large majority—though it commanded more than five votes in the Assembly to every two of the Opposition—yet within three years both leaders had withdrawn from public life, and Baldwin himself had sustained a personal defeat at the polls. The Liberal Government, reconstituted under Sir Francis Hincks, managed to retain office for three years more; but it was crippled throughout its whole term by the most bitter internecine feuds, and it fell {21} at length before the assaults of those who had been elected to support it. The measure responsible more than any other for the excited and bitter feeling which prevailed was the Rebellion Losses Bill. There is reason to believe that the members of the Government, or at any rate the Upper-Canadian ministers, were not at any time united in their support of the Bill. But the French vehemently insisted on it, and the Ministry, dependent as it was on the Lower-Canadian vote for its existence, had no choice. The Bill provided, as the title indicates, for compensation out of the public treasury to those persons in Lower Canada who had suffered loss of property during the rebellion. It was not proposed to make a distinction between loyalists and rebels, further than by the insertion of a provision that no person who had actually been convicted of treason, or who had been transported to Bermuda, should share in the indemnity. Now, a large number of the people of Lower Canada had been more or less concerned in the rebellion, but not one-tenth of them had been arrested, and only a small minority of those arrested had been brought to trial. It is therefore easy to see that the proposal was calculated {22} to produce a bitter feeling among those who looked upon rebellion as the most grievous of crimes. It was, they argued, simply putting a premium on treason. The measure was fiercely resisted by the Opposition, and called forth a lively and acrimonious debate. Among its strongest opponents was Macdonald. According to his custom, he listened patiently to the arguments for and against the measure, and did not make his speech until towards the close of the debate.

Despite the protests of the Opposition, the Bill passed its third reading in the House of Assembly on March 9, 1849, by a vote of forty-seven to eighteen. Outside the walls of parliament the clamour grew fiercer every hour. Meetings were held all over Upper Canada and in Montreal, and petitions to Lord Elgin, the governor-general, poured in thick and fast, praying that the obnoxious measure might not become law. In Toronto some disturbances took place, during which the houses of Baldwin, Blake, and other prominent Liberals were attacked, and the Reform leaders were burned in effigy.

The Government, which all along seems to have underrated public feeling, was so unfortunate as to incur the suspicion of {23} deliberately going out of its way to inflame popular resentment. It was considered expedient, for commercial reasons, to bring into operation immediately a customs law, and the Ministry took the unwise course of advising the governor-general to assent to the Rebellion Losses Bill at the same time. Accordingly, on April 25, Lord Elgin proceeded to the Parliament Buildings and gave the royal assent to these and other bills. Not a suspicion of the governor's intention had got abroad until the morning of the eventful day. His action was looked upon as a defiance of public sentiment; the popular mind was already violently excited, and consequences of the direst kind followed. His Excellency, when returning to his residence, 'Monklands,' was grossly insulted, his carriage was almost shattered by stones, and he himself narrowly escaped bodily injury at the hands of the infuriated populace. A public meeting was held that evening on the Champs de Mars, and resolutions were adopted praying Her Majesty to recall Lord Elgin. But no mere passing of resolutions would suffice the fiercer spirits of that meeting. The cry arose—'To the Parliament Buildings!' and soon the lurid flames mounting on the night air told {24} the horror-stricken people of Montreal that anarchy was in their midst. The whole building, including the legislative libraries, which contained many rare and priceless records of the colony, was destroyed in a few minutes.

This abominable outrage called for the severest censure, not merely on the rioters, but also on the authorities, who took few steps to avert the calamity. An eyewitness stated that half a dozen men could have extinguished the fire, which owed its origin to lighted balls of paper thrown about the chamber by the rioters; but there does not seem to have been even a policeman on the ground. Four days afterwards the Government, still disregarding public sentiment, brought the governor-general to town to receive an address voted to him by the Assembly. The occasion was the signal for another disturbance. Stones were thrown at Lord Elgin's carriage; and missiles of a more offensive character were directed with such correctness of aim that the ubiquitous reporter of the day described the back of the governor's carriage as 'presenting an awful sight.' Various societies, notably St Andrew's Society of Montreal, passed resolutions removing Lord Elgin from the presidency or patronage of their {25} organizations; some of them formally expelled him. On the other hand, he received many addresses from various parts of the country expressive of confidence and esteem. Sir Allan MacNab and William Cayley repaired to England to protest, on behalf of the Opposition, against the governor's course. They were closely followed by Francis Hincks, representing the Government. The matter duly came up in the Imperial parliament. In the House of Commons the Bill was vigorously attacked by Gladstone, who shared the view of the Canadian Opposition that it was a measure for the rewarding of rebels. It was defended by Lord John Russell, and Lord Elgin's course in following the advice of his ministers was ultimately approved by the home government.

As in many another case, the expectation proved worse than the reality. The commission appointed by the Government under the Rebellion Losses Act was composed of moderate men, who had the wisdom to refuse compensation to many claimants on the ground of their having been implicated in the rebellion, although never convicted by any court. Had it been understood that the restricted interpretation which the commission gave the Bill would be applied, it is possible that this {26} disgraceful episode in the history of Canada would not have to be told.

An inevitable consequence of this lamentable occurrence was the removal of the seat of government from Montreal. The Administration felt that, in view of what had taken place, it would be folly to expose the Government and parliament to a repetition of these outrages. This resolve gave rise to innumerable jealousies on the part of the several cities which aspired to the honour of having the legislature in their midst. Macdonald was early on the look-out, and, at the conclusion of his speech on the disturbances, in the course of which he severely censured the Ministry for its neglect to take ordinary precautions to avert what it should have known was by no means an unlikely contingency, he moved that the seat of government be restored to Kingston—a motion which was defeated by a large majority, as was a similar proposal in favour of Bytown (Ottawa). It was finally determined to adopt the ambulatory system of having the capital alternately at Quebec and Toronto, a system which prevailed until the removal to Ottawa in 1865.[4]

{27}

The historic Annexation manifesto of 1849 was an outcome of the excitement produced by the Rebellion Losses Act. Several hundreds of the leading citizens of Montreal, despairing of the future of a country which could tolerate such legislation as they had recently witnessed, affixed their names to a document advocating a friendly and peaceable separation from British connection as a prelude to union with the United States. Men subsequently known as Sir John Rose, Sir John Caldwell Abbott, Sir Francis Johnson, Sir David Macpherson, together with such well-known citizens as the Redpaths, the Molsons, the Torrances, and the Workmans, were among the number.

Macdonald, referring in later years to this Annexation manifesto, observed:

Our fellows lost their heads. I was pressed to sign it, but refused and advocated the formation of the British America League as a more sensible procedure. From all parts of Upper Canada, and from the British section of Lower Canada, and {28} from the British inhabitants of Montreal, representatives were chosen. They met at Kingston for the purpose of considering the great danger to which the constitution of Canada was exposed. A safety-valve was found. Our first resolution was that we were resolved to maintain inviolate the connection with the mother country. The second proposition was that the true solution of the difficulty lay in the confederation of all the provinces. The third resolution was that we should attempt to form in such confederation, or in Canada before Confederation, a commercial national policy. The effects of the formation of the British America League were marvellous. Under its influence the annexation sentiment disappeared, the feeling of irritation died away, and the principles which were laid down by the British America

League in 1850 are the lines on which the Conservative-Liberal party has moved ever since.

The carrying of the Rebellion Losses Bill was the high-water mark of the LaFontaine-Baldwin Administration. In the following session symptoms of disintegration began to {29} appear. Grown bold by success, the advanced section of the Upper-Canadian Radicals pressed for the immediate secularization of the Clergy Reserves[5] by a process scarcely distinguishable from confiscation. To this demand the Government was not prepared to agree, and in consequence there was much disaffection in the Reform ranks. This had its counterpart in Lower Canada, where Louis Joseph Papineau and his *Parti Rouge* clamoured for various impracticable constitutional changes, including a general application of the elective principle, a republican form of government, and, ultimately, annexation to the United States.

To add to the difficulties of the situation, George Brown, in the columns of the *Globe*, which up to this time was supposed to reflect the views of the Government, began a furious onslaught against Roman Catholicism in general and on the French Canadians in particular. This fatuous course could not fail to prove embarrassing to a Ministry which drew its main support from Lower Canada. {30} It was the time of the 'Papal Aggression' in England. Anti-Catholicism was in the air, and found a congenial exponent in George Brown, whose vehement and intolerant nature espoused the new crusade with enthusiasm. It is difficult for any one living in our day to conceive of the leading organ of a great political party writing thus of a people who at that time numbered very nearly one-half the population of Canada, and from whose ranks the parliamentary supporters of its own political party were largely drawn:

It would give us great pleasure to think that the French Canadians were really hearty coadjutors of the Upper-Canadian Reformers, but all the indications point the other way, and it appears hoping against hope to anticipate still; their race, their religion, their habits, their ignorance, are all against it, and their recent conduct is in harmony with these.[6]

The Ministry could not be expected to stand this sort of thing indefinitely. They were {31} compelled to disavow the *Globe*, and so to widen the breach between them and Brown.

In 1851 Baldwin and LaFontaine retired from public life. A new Administration was formed from the same party under the leadership of Hincks and Morin, and in the general elections that followed George Brown was returned to parliament for Kent. The new Ministry, however, found no more favour at the hands of Brown than did its predecessor. Nor was Brown content to confine his attacks to the floor of the House. He wrote and published in the *Globe* a series of open letters addressed to Hincks, charging him with having paltered away his Liberal principles for the sake of French-Canadian support. To such lengths did Brown carry his opposition, that in the general elections of 1854 we find him, together with the extreme Liberals, known as Rouges, in Lower Canada, openly supporting the Conservative leaders against the Government.

While Brown was thus helping on the disruption of his party, his future great rival, by a very different line of conduct, was laying broad and deep the foundations of a policy tending to ameliorate the racial and religious differences unfortunately existing between {32} Upper and Lower Canada.[7] To a man of Macdonald's large and generous mind the fierce intolerance of Brown must have been in itself most distasteful. At the same time, there is no doubt that George Brown's anti-Catholic, anti-French crusade, while but one factor among several in contributing to the downfall of the Baldwin and Hincks Governments, became in after years, when directed against successive Liberal-Conservative Administrations, the most formidable obstacle against which Macdonald had to contend.

The result of the *Globe's* propaganda amounted to this, that for twenty years the Conservative leader found himself in a large minority in his own province of Upper Canada, and dependent upon Lower Canada for support—truly an unsatisfactory state of affairs to himself personally, and one most inimical to the welfare of the country. It was not pleasant for a public man to be condemned, election after election, to fight a losing battle {33} in his home province, where he was best known, and to be obliged to carry his measures by the vote of his allies of another province. It is therefore not to be wondered at that Sir John Macdonald in his reminiscent moods sometimes alluded to these days, thus:

Had I but consented to take the popular side in Upper Canada, I could have ridden the Protestant horse much better than George Brown, and could have had an overwhelming majority. But I willingly sacrificed my own popularity for the good of the country, and did equal justice to all men.[8]

Scattered throughout his correspondence are several references of a similar tenor. I do not believe, however, that the temptation ever seriously assailed him. Indeed, we find that at every step in his career, when the opportunity presented itself for showing sympathy with the French Canadians in their struggle for the maintenance of their just rights, he invariably espoused their cause, not then a popular one. At the union of Upper and Lower Canada in 1841 there seems to have been a general disposition to hasten the {34} absorption of the French-Canadian people, so confidently predicted by Lord Durham. That nobleman declared with the utmost frankness that, in his opinion, the French Canadians were destined speedily to lose their distinctive nationality by becoming merged in the Anglo-Saxon communities surrounding them, and he conceived that nothing would conduce so effectually to this result as the union of Upper and Lower Canada. His successor, Lord Sydenham, evidently shared these views upon the subject, for his Cabinet did not contain a single French Canadian. In furtherance of this policy it was provided in the Union Act (1840) that all the proceedings of parliament should be printed in the English language only. At that time the French Canadians numbered more than one-half the people of Canada, and the great majority of them knew no other language than French. No wonder that this provision was felt by them to be a hardship, or that it tended to embitter them and to increase their hostility to the Union. Macdonald had not sat in parliament a month before the Government of which he was a supporter proposed and carried in the House of Assembly a resolution providing for the removal of this restriction. {35} During the ensuing two years the same Government opened negotiations (which came to nothing at the time) with certain leaders among the French Canadians looking towards political co-operation, and similar though equally fruitless overtures were made to them during the weeks following Macdonald's admission into the Draper Cabinet. This policy Macdonald had deliberately adopted and carried with him into Opposition.

In a letter outlining the political campaign of 1854, he says in so many words:

My belief is that there must be a material alteration in the character of the new House. I believe also that there must be a change of Ministry after the election, and, *from my friendly relations with the French*, I am inclined to believe my assistance would be sought.[9]

Meanwhile the cleavage in the Reform ranks was daily becoming wider. Indeed, as has been said, the Radical section of the Upper-Canadian representation, known as the Clear Grit party, were frequently to be found voting with the Conservative Opposition, with whom they had nothing in common save dislike and {36} distrust of the Government. The result of the elections of 1854 showed that no one of the three parties — the Ministerialists, the Opposition, or the Clear Grits and Lower-Canadian Rouges combined — had an independent majority. Upon one point, however, the two last-named groups were equally determined, namely, the defeat of the Government. This they promptly effected by a junction of forces. The leader of the regular Opposition, Sir Allan MacNab, was 'sent for.' But his following did not exceed forty, while the defeated party numbered fifty-five, and the extreme Radicals about thirty-five. It was obvious that no Ministry could be formed exclusively from one party; it was equally clear that the government of the country must be carried on. In these circumstances Sir Allan resolved upon trying his hand at forming a new Government. He first offered Macdonald the attorney-generalship for Upper Canada, and, availing himself of his young ally's 'friendly relations with the French,' entered into negotiations with A. N. Morin, the leader of the Lower-Canadian wing of the late Cabinet. Morin consented to serve in the new Ministry. The followers of MacNab and Morin together formed a majority of the {37} House. The French leader, however, was most anxious that his late allies in Upper Canada—Sir Francis Hincks and his friends—should be parties to the coalition. Hincks, while not seeing his way to join the new Administration, expressed his approval of the arrangements, and promised his support on the understanding that two of his political friends from Upper Canada should have seats in the new Government. This proposal was accepted by Mac-Nab, and John Ross (son-in-law of Baldwin) and Thomas Spence were chosen. The basis of the coalition was an agreement to carry out the principal measures foreshadowed in the speech from the throne—including the abolition of the Seigneurial Tenure[10] and the secularization of the Clergy Reserves.

SIR ALLAN NAPIER MACNAB

From a portrait in the John Ross Robertson Collection,
Toronto Public Library

Sir Allan Napier MacNab.
From a portrait in the John Ross Robertson Collection,
Toronto Public Library

Such was the beginning of the great Liberal-Conservative party which almost constantly from 1854 to 1896 controlled the destinies of Canada. Its history has singularly borne out the contention of its founders, that in uniting as they did at a time when their co-operation was essential to the conduct of affairs, they {38} acted in the best interests of the country. For a long time there had not been any real sympathy between the French Liberal leaders, LaFontaine and Morin, and the Liberals of Upper Canada. After the echoes of the rebellion had died away these French Liberals became in reality the Conservatives of Lower Canada. The *Globe* repeatedly declared this. Their junction with MacNab and Macdonald was therefore a fusion rather than a coalition. The latter word more correctly describes the union between the Conservatives and the Moderate Reformers of Upper Canada. It was, however, a coalition abundantly justified by circumstances. The principal charge brought against the Conservative party at the time was that in pledging themselves to secularize the Clergy Reserves they were guilty of an abandonment of principle. But in 1854 this had ceased to be a party question. The progress of events had rendered it inevitable that these lands should be made available for settlement; and since this had to come, it was better that the change should be brought about by men who had already striven to preserve the rights of property acquired under the Clergy Reserve grants, rather than by those whose policy was little {39} short of spoliation. The propriety and reasonableness of all this was very generally recognized at the time, not merely by the supporters of MacNab and Macdonald, but also by their political opponents. A. A. Dorion, the Rouge leader, considered the alliance quite natural. Robert Baldwin and Francis Hincks both publicly defended it, and their course did much to cement the union between the Conservatives and those who, forty years after the events here set down, were known to the older members of the community as 'Baldwin Reformers.'

[1] The question of the authorship of Lord Durham's Report is one which all Canadians have heard debated from their youth up. No matter who may have composed the document, it was Lord Durham's opinions and principles that it expressed. Lord Durham signed it and took responsibility for it, and it very naturally and properly goes under his name. But in a review of my *Memoirs of Sir John Macdonald* the *Athenaeum* (January 12, 1895) said: 'He,' the author, 'repeats at second hand, and with the incorrectness of those who do not take the trouble to verify their references, that Lord Durham's report on Canada' was written by the nobleman whose name it bears. 'He could easily have ascertained that the author of the report which he commends was Charles Buller, two paragraphs excepted which were contributed by Gibbon Wakefield and R. D. Hanson.' Some years later, however, in a review of Mr Stuart Reid's book on Lord Durham, the same *Athenaeum* (November 3, 1906) observed: 'Mr Reid conclusively disposes of Brougham's malignant slander that the matter of Lord Durham's report on Canada came from a felon (Wakefield) and the style from a coxcomb (Buller). The latter, in his account of the mission, frequently alludes to the report, but not a single phrase hints that he was the author.'

[2] 'It is well known, sir, that while I have always been a member of what is called the Conservative party, I could never have been called a Tory, although there is no man who more respects what is called old-fogey Toryism than I do, so long as it is based upon principle' (Speech of Hon. John A. Macdonald at St Thomas, 1860).

[3] 'In '47 I was a member of the Canadian Government, and we went to a general election knowing well that we should be defeated' (Sir John A. Macdonald to the Hon. P. C. Hill, dated Ottawa, October 7, 1867).

[4] The dates of the first meetings of the Executive Council, held at the various seats of government, from the Union in 1841 till 1867, are as follows: at Kingston, June 11, 1841; at Montreal, July 1, 1844; at Toronto, November 13, 1849; at Quebec, October 22, 1851; at Toronto, November 9, 1855; at Quebec, October 21, 1859; at Ottawa, November 28, 1865.

[5] That is, that the land set apart by the Constitutional Act of 1791 'for the support and maintenance of a Protestant Clergy,'

amounting to one-seventh of all the lands granted, should be taken over by the Government and thrown open for settlement.

[6] *Globe*, 1851. For further instances see *Globe*, February 9 and December 14, 1853; February 9, 18, 22 and November 5, 1856; August 7 and December 23, 1857.

[7] To all Conservatives who cherish the memory of Sir John Macdonald we bring the reminder that no leader ever opposed so sternly the attempt to divide this community on racial or religious lines' (*Globe*, November 10, 1900).

The *Globe's* latter-day estimate of Sir John Macdonald recalls the late Tom Reid's definition of a statesman — 'a successful politician who is dead.'

[8] To a friend, dated Ottawa, April 20, 1869.

[9] See Pope's *Memoirs of Sir John Macdonald*, vol. i, p. 103.

[10] The seigneurial system was a survival of the French régime. The reader is referred to *The Seigneurs of Old Canada* by Professor Munro in the present Series.

{40}

CHAPTER II

MIDDLE LIFE

The Liberal-Conservative Government formed in 1854 was destined to a long and successful career, though not without the usual inevitable changes. Very shortly after its accession to power, Lord Elgin, whose term of office had expired, was succeeded by Sir Edmund Head. The new governor-general was a man of rare scholastic attainments. During the previous seven years he had occupied the position of lieutenant-governor of New Brunswick, and he was to administer, for a like period, the public affairs of Canada acceptably and well. One thing, however, greatly interfered with his popularity and lessened his usefulness. A story was spread abroad that Sir Edmund Head had called the French Canadians 'an inferior race.' This, though it was not true, was often reiterated; and the French Canadians persisted in believing that Sir Edmund had made the remark—even after an explanation of what he really did say.

{41}

Early in 1855 Morin retired to the bench. His place in the Cabinet was filled by George Étienne Cartier, member for Verchères in the Assembly. Cartier had begun his political career in 1848 as a supporter of LaFontaine, but he was one of those who followed Morin in his alliance with the Conservatives. Now, on the withdrawal of his chief, he succeeded, in effect, to the leadership of the French-Canadian wing of the Government. The corresponding position from the English province was held by John A. Macdonald, for it was no secret at the time that Sir Allan MacNab, the titular leader, had seen his best days, and leaned heavily upon his friend the attorney-general for Upper Canada.

Under these circumstances were brought together the two men who for the ensuing eighteen years governed the country almost without intermission. During the whole of this long period they were, with but one trivial misunderstanding, intimate personal friends. That Sir John Macdonald entertained the warmest feelings of unbroken regard for his colleague, I know, for he told me so many times; and Cartier's correspondence plainly indicates that these sentiments were fully reciprocated.

{42}

Sir George Cartier was a man who devoted his whole life to the public service of his country. He was truthful, honest, and sincere, and commanded the respect and confidence of all with whom he came in contact. Had it not been for Sir George Cartier, it is doubtful whether the Dominion of Canada would exist to-day. He it was who faced at its inception the not unnatural French-Canadian distrust of the measure. It was his magnificent courage and resistless energy which triumphed over all opposition. Confederation was not the work of any one person. Macdonald, Brown, Tupper—each played his indispensable part; but assuredly not the least important share in the accomplishment of that great undertaking is to be ascribed to George Étienne Cartier.

SIR EDMUND WALKER HEAD

From the John Ross Robertson Collection, Toronto Public Library

**Sir Edmund Walker Head.
From the John Ross Robertson Collection,
Toronto Public Library**

Other public men of the period claim our brief attention. Sir Allan MacNab, the leader of the Conservative party, had had a long and diversified experience. He was born at Niagara in 1798, and at an early age took up the profession of arms. When the Americans attacked Toronto in 1813, Allan MacNab, then a boy at school, was one of a number selected to carry a musket. He afterwards entered the Navy and was rated as a {43} midshipman on board Sir James Yeo's ship on the Great Lakes. MacNab subsequently joined the 100th Regiment under Colonel Murray, and was engaged in the storming of Niagara. He was a member and speaker of the old House of Assembly of Upper Canada, and in 1841 was elected to the first parliament under the new Union. For sixteen years he continued to represent Hamilton, serving during a portion of the time as speaker of the Assembly. In 1860 he was elected a member of the Legislative Council, and was chosen speaker of that body a few months prior to his death in 1862. In 1854, as we have seen, he was called upon, as the recognized leader of the Opposition, to form the new Ministry. He thus became prime minister, an event that caused some grumbling on the part of younger spirits who thought Sir Allan rather a 'back number.' It has been charged against Sir John Macdonald that he at the time intrigued to accomplish his old chief's overthrow, but there is not a particle of truth in the statement. When forming his plans for the general elections of 1854, Macdonald thus wrote:

You say truly that we are a good deal hampered with 'old blood.' Sir Allan {44} will not be in our way, however. He is very reasonable, and requires only that we should not in his 'sere and yellow leaf' offer him the indignity of casting him aside. This I would never assent to, for I cannot forget his services in days gone by.[1]

Sir Allan was a Tory of the 'Family Compact' school, which with changed conditions was fast becoming an anachronism. He was at the same time a loyal and faithful public servant.

MacNab retired from the premiership in 1856 and was succeeded by Colonel (afterwards Sir) Étienne Taché, who had held Cabinet office continuously since 1848. Taché was a more moderate man than Sir Allan, without his ambition or intractability; but he does not appear to have been distinguished by any particular aptitude for public life, and the prominence he attained was in large measure the result of circumstance. He was, however, generally regarded as a safe man with no private interests to serve, and he was quite content to allow Macdonald and Cartier a free hand in the direction of public affairs. {45} Under their united guidance much was accomplished. During the first session after the formation of the Liberal-Conservative party the two great questions which had long distracted the united province of Canada—the Clergy Reserves and the Seigneurial Tenure—were settled on terms which were accounted satisfactory by all moderate and reasonable men. Both the measures which the Government introduced to adjust these matters were opposed at every stage by Brown, Dorion, and other professed champions of the popular will.[2] Brown, who had never forgotten the failure of the Conservative leaders to open negotiations with him on the defeat of the Hincks Government, vented his wrath alternately on the new Ministry and on the Roman Catholic Church, assailing both with amazing violence. Despite this unrestrained vehemence, impulsiveness, and lack of discretion, George Brown's great ability and intellectual power made him a formidable opponent, as the ministers learned to their cost.

{46} Meanwhile, as the different groups settled into their places, political parties in the legislature became more clearly defined. The French-Canadian ministerialists soon ceased to be regarded as anything but Conservatives; and while many of the Upper-Canadian supporters of the Government long continued to be known as 'Baldwin Reformers,' the line of separation between them and their Conservative allies grew fainter every day. It was inevitable that this should be so. Baldwin himself had disappeared. Hincks had left the country. John Ross, the leading member of the Liberal wing of the coalition, had resigned from the Cabinet. So it came to pass, after the withdrawal of Sir Allan MacNab, that many quondam Liberals grew to realize that there was no longer any reason why they should not unite under the leadership of the man who inspired equally the confidence and the regard of the whole party.

All this was gall and wormwood to Brown, who pursued Macdonald with a malignity which has no parallel in our happier times. Nor, it must be confessed, did Macdonald fail to retort. Though not a resentful person, nor one who could not control his feelings, he never disguised his personal antipathy {47} towards the man who had persistently and for many years misrepresented and traduced him. On one occasion Macdonald was moved to bring certain accusations against Brown's personal character. These, however, he failed to establish to the satisfaction of the special committee of parliament appointed to try the charge. This was the only time, as far as I know, when Brown got the better of his rival.

While the Liberal-Conservative forces were being consolidated under Macdonald and Cartier, a similar process was taking place in the Reform ranks under Dorion and Brown. Dorion was a distinguished member of the Montreal bar and a courtly and polished gentleman of unblemished reputation. He had become the leading member of the *Parti Rouge* on Papineau's retirement in 1854, and was now the chief of the few French Radicals in the Assembly. In like manner Brown assumed the leadership of the Clear Grits, the Radicals of Upper Canada.

While the politicians were thus busy, Canada continued to develop, if not at the rate to which we are accustomed in these later days, still at a fair pace. In 1851 the population of Upper Canada had been 952,000 and {48} that of Lower Canada 890,000. Of the cities Montreal boasted 58,000, Quebec 42,000, Toronto 31,000, and Kingston 12,000. By 1861 these figures had grown to 1,396,000 for Upper Canada, 1,111,000 for Lower Canada, and the cities had correspondingly increased. Montreal had now 90,000 people, Quebec 51,000, Toronto 45,000, and Kingston 14,000. The total revenue of Canada in 1855 amounted to $4,870,000, not half that of the single province of Ontario to-day, and the expenditure to $4,780,000.

Much had already been spent on the improvement of inland navigation, and the early fifties saw the beginning of a great advance in railway construction. The Intercolonial Railway to connect the Maritime Provinces with Canada was projected as early as in 1846, though inability to agree upon the route delayed construction many years. In 1853 the Grand Trunk was opened from Montreal to Portland in Maine. The Great Western (now a portion of the Grand Trunk system), running between the Niagara and Detroit rivers, was opened during the following year; and 1855 witnessed the completion of the Grand Trunk from Montreal to Brockville, and the Great Western from Toronto to {49} Hamilton. The Detroit river at that time marked the western limit of settlement in Canada. North and west stretched a vast lone land about which scarcely anything was known. The spirit of enterprise, however, was stirring. The expiry of certain trading privileges granted to the Hudson's Bay Company in 1838 offered the occasion for an inquiry by a committee of the Imperial House of Commons into the claims of the company to the immense region associated with its name. The Canadian Government accepted an invitation to be represented at this investigation, and in the early part of the year 1857 dispatched to England Chief Justice Draper as commissioner. The committee, which included such eminent persons as Lord John Russell, Lord Derby, and Mr Gladstone, reported to the effect that terms should be agreed upon between the company and the Imperial and Canadian governments, in order that the territory might be made available for settlement; but no further steps were then taken. The question was not to be settled until some years later.

About the same time certain adventurous spirits approached the Canadian Government with a suggestion to build a railway across {50} the prairies and through the Rocky mountains to the Pacific ocean. From Sir John Macdonald's papers it appears that a proposal of this nature was made to him in the early part of 1858. There is a letter addressed to Macdonald, dated at Kingston in January of that year, and signed 'Walter R. Jones.' In the light of subsequent events this letter is interesting. The writer suggests that the time has arrived to organize a company to build a railway 'through British American territory to the Pacific.' It would be some years, of course, before such a company could actually begin the work of construction; therefore action should begin at once. Nothing will be gained by delay, the writer points out; and if Canada does not seize the golden opportunity, it is probable that the United States will be first in the field with such a railway, 'as they are fully alive to the great benefit it would be to them, not only locally, but as a highway from Europe to China, India, and Australia.' This would greatly lessen the value of a Canadian and British railway, and would cause the enterprise to 'be delayed or entirely abandoned.' Thus Canada would lose, not only the through traffic and business of the railway, but also the {51} opportunity to open up the Great West to settlers, 'which of itself would be a great boon to Canada.'

The letter proceeds to say that, as the claims of the Hudson's Bay Company to the lands of the West are shortly to be extinguished, the railway company could secure the grant of a harbour on Vancouver Island and the privilege of 'working the coal mines there'; also, 'a grant of land along the proposed line of railway.' A subsidy should be obtained from the Imperial Government for 'a line of steamers from Vancouver Island to China, India, and Australia.' If the Canadian people would take up the matter with spirit and buy largely of the stock, and if the subject were laid before the merchants of London, 'there would be no difficulty in raising the required capital, say £15,000,000.' There can be no doubt that the line would pay. Any one looking at a map of the world can see that it would afford the shortest route between Europe and the East. The writer thinks that it would be well to start the nucleus of a company immediately so as to apply for a charter at the next session of the Canadian parliament. 'Of course,' he adds, 'in my humble circumstances it would be the height of folly to think of attempting {52} to organize or connect myself with such a vast undertaking unless I could get the countenance and support of some one in high standing.' Macdonald, however, deemed the proposal premature until the claims of the Hudson's Bay Company were disposed of. He was destined to carry it out many years later.

The question as to the seat of government proved in those days extremely troublesome, promising to vie with the now happily removed Clergy Reserves question, in frequently recurring to cause difficulty. The inconvenience of the ambulatory system under which the legislature sat alternately four years at Quebec and four years at Toronto was acknowledged by everybody, but it seemed impossible to agree upon any one place for the capital. Quebec, Montreal, Toronto, and Kingston all aspired to the honour, and the sectional jealousies among the supporters of the Ministry afforded periodical opportunities to the Opposition, of which they did not fail to take advantage. One ministerial crisis arising out of this dispute acquired exceptional prominence by reason of the fact that it led to what is known in Canadian history as the 'Double Shuffle.'

{53}

In the session of 1857 the Ministry proposed to submit the question to the personal decision of the queen, and introduced resolutions in the Assembly praying that Her Majesty would be graciously pleased to exercise the royal prerogative by the selection of some one place as the permanent capital of Canada. This reference to Her Majesty was fiercely opposed by the Clear Grits as being a tacit acknowledgment of Canada's unfitness to exercise that responsible government for which she had contended so long. The *Globe*, in a series of articles, denounced the 'very idea as degradation.' The motion was nevertheless carried by a substantial majority, and the address went home accordingly.

The harvest of 1857 proved a failure, and in the autumn of that year Canada passed through one of the most severe periods of financial depression with which she has ever been afflicted. The period between 1854 and 1856 saw great commercial activity. Vast sums of money had been spent in constructing railways. This outlay, three bountiful harvests, and the abnormally high prices of farm products caused by the Crimean War, combined to make a period of almost unexampled prosperity—a prosperity more {54} apparent than real. The usual reaction followed. Peace in Europe, coinciding with a bad harvest in Canada, produced the inevitable result. Every class and interest felt the strain. Nor did the Ministry escape. It was at this gloomy period that Colonel Taché, weary of office, relinquished the cares of state, and Macdonald became first minister. Two days after the new Ministry had taken office parliament was dissolved and writs were issued for a general election. The main issues in this contest, both forced by George Brown, were 'Representation by Population' and 'Non-sectarian Schools'—otherwise No Popery. These cries told with much effect in Upper Canada. 'Rep. by Pop.,' as it was familiarly called, had long been a favourite policy with Brown and the *Globe*. By the Union Act of 1840 the representation of Upper and Lower Canada in the Assembly was fixed at eighty-four, forty-two from each province. At that time Lower Canada had the advantage of population, and consequently a smaller representation than that to which it would have been entitled on the basis of numbers. But the French Canadians were content to abide by the compact, and on that score there was peace. As soon, however, as {55} the influx of settlers into Upper Canada turned the scale, the *Globe* began to agitate for a revision of the agreement. In the session of 1853 Brown condemned the system of equal representation, and moved that the representation of the people in parliament should be based upon population, without regard to any line of separation between Upper and Lower Canada. On this he was defeated, but with rare pertinacity he stuck to his guns, and urged his views upon the Assembly at every opportune and inopportune moment. The Macdonald-Cartier Government opposed the principle of representation by population because it was not in accord with the Union Act. That Act was a distinct bargain between Upper Canada and Lower Canada, and could not be altered without the consent of both. On the school question Macdonald took the ground that the clause granting separate schools to Roman Catholics was in the Common School Act long before he became a member of the government—having been placed there by Robert Baldwin—and that it would be unfair and unjust arbitrarily to take the privilege away. Moreover, he argued, on the authority of Egerton Ryerson, a Protestant clergyman and superintendent of {56} schools for Upper Canada, that the offending clause injured nobody, but, on the contrary, 'widens the basis of the common school system.'

This might be good logic, and inherently fair and just. All the same, the *Globe* conducted its campaign with such telling effect that three ministers lost their seats in the general elections of 1857, and the Clear Grits came out of the campaign in Upper Canada with a majority of six or eight.

In Lower Canada there was a different result. The appeals to sectional and religious prejudice, which wrought havoc in the ranks of the ministerial supporters in the upper province, had a contrary effect among the Rouges. Their alliance with the Clear Grit party wellnigh brought their complete overthrow. Dorion himself was elected, but his namesake J. B. E. Dorion, commonly known as *l'enfant terrible*, was unsuccessful, as also was Luther H. Holton, the leading English-speaking Liberal of the province. Other prominent Rouges such as Papin, Doutre, Fournier, and Letellier were given abundant leisure to deplore the fanaticism of George Brown. Cartier had the satisfaction of coming to the assistance of his colleague with {57} almost the whole representation of Lower Canada at his back.

This brings us to the historic incident of the 'Double Shuffle.' Shortly after the elections it became known that Her Majesty, in response to the request of the legislature, had chosen Ottawa as the seat of government. The announcement was somewhat prematurely made and gave rise to a good deal of dissatisfaction. This manifested itself when parliament met. In the early days of the session of 1858 a motion was carried in the Assembly to the effect that 'in the opinion of this House, the city of Ottawa ought not to be the permanent seat of government of this province.' Thereupon the Ministry promptly resigned, construing the vote as a slight upon Her Majesty, who had been asked to make the selection. The governor-general then sent for Brown and invited him to form a new Administration. What followed affords an admirable illustration of the character of George Brown. Though in an undoubted minority in a House fresh from the people, with Lower Canada almost unitedly opposed to him, Brown accepted the invitation of the governor-general. His only hope could have lain in a dissolution, and Sir Edmund Head {58} gave him to understand at the outset, both verbally and in writing, that on this he must not count. There are several examples in British political history, notably that of Lord Derby in 1858 and Disraeli in 1873, where statesmen in opposition, feeling that the occasion was not ripe for their purposes, have refused to take advantage of the defeat of the Ministry to which they were opposed. George Brown was not so constituted. Without attempting to weigh the chances of being able to maintain himself in power for a single week, he eagerly grasped the prize. Two days after his summons he and his colleagues were sworn into office and had assumed the functions of advisers of the crown. How accurately does this headlong impetuosity bear out Sir John Macdonald's estimate of the man![3]

The inevitable happened, and that speedily. Within a few hours the Assembly passed a vote of want of confidence in the new Ministry, and Brown and his colleagues, having been refused a dissolution, were compelled to resign. The governor-general sent for A. T. Galt, then {59} the able and popular member of the House from Sherbrooke in Lower Canada. But Galt declined the honour. The formation of a new Administration was then entrusted to Cartier, who, with the assistance of Macdonald, soon accomplished the task. Thus came into power the former Macdonald-Cartier Government, under the changed name of the Cartier-Macdonald Government, with personnel very slightly altered. Even this did not fill up the cup of Brown's humiliation. By their acceptance of office he and his colleagues had vacated their seats in the Assembly, and so found themselves outside the legislature for the remainder of the session. Those members of the Cartier-Macdonald Government, on the contrary, who had been members of the Macdonald-Cartier Government, did not vacate their seats by reason of their resumption of office. The Independence of Parliament Act of 1857 provided that

whenever any person holding the office of Receiver General, Inspector General, Secretary of the Province, Commissioner of Crown Lands, Attorney General, Solicitor General, Commissioner of Public Works, Speaker of the Legislative Council, {60} President of Committees of the Executive Council, Minister of Agriculture, or Postmaster General, and being at the same time a member of the Legislative Assembly or an elected member of the Legislative Council, shall resign his office, and within one month after his resignation accept any other of the said offices, he shall not thereby vacate his seat in the said Assembly or Council.

These words are clear. Any member of a government could resign his office and accept another within one month without vacating his seat in parliament. Thirty days had not elapsed since Macdonald had held the portfolio of attorney-general. There was, therefore, no legal necessity for his taking the sense of his constituents on resuming it. Elections no more in 1858 than now were run for the fun of the thing. One technical objection alone stood in the way. The Act says that if any member resign office, and within one month after his resignation accept *any other* of the said offices, he shall not thereby vacate his seat in the Assembly. It says nothing about the effect of accepting anew the office just demitted, though it seems only reasonable {61} to infer that, if the acceptance of a new office by a minister did not call for a fresh appeal to his constituents, *a fortiori* neither would the mere resumption of an office whose acceptance they had already approved. In the judgment of Macdonald and several of his colleagues there was no legal impediment to the direct resumption of their former offices, but a difference of opinion existed on the point, and, in order to keep clearly within the law, the ministers first accepted portfolios other than those formerly held by them. Thus, Cartier was first sworn in as inspector-general and Macdonald as postmaster-general. On the following day they resigned these portfolios and were appointed respectively to their old offices of attorney-general East and attorney-general West. Their colleagues in the Macdonald-Cartier Government underwent a similar experience.

The 'Double Shuffle' proved a source of acute dissatisfaction to Brown and his friends. The ministers were accused by them of having perverted an Act of Parliament to a sense it was never intended to bear. Their action in swearing to discharge duties which they never intended to perform was characterized as little short of perjury. They were, however, {62} sustained both by parliament and in the courts. Thirteen years later, no less a personage than Gladstone gave to the proceeding the sanction of his great authority. In order to qualify Sir Robert Collier, his attorney-general, for a seat on the Judicial Committee of the Privy Council, appointments to which were restricted to judges, he nominated him a justice of the Court of Common Pleas, in which Sir Robert took his seat, sat for a few days, resigned, and went on the Judicial Committee.[4]

The year 1858 saw the beginnings of a movement in the direction of Confederation. At an early period in the session Galt raised the question in an interesting speech. When he joined the Ministry, as inspector-general (finance minister), he again brought it forward. During recess a delegation consisting of Cartier, Galt, and John Ross proceeded to England with the object of discussing the subject with Her Majesty's government.

{63}

The ranks of the Reform Opposition at this time included D'Arcy M'Gee, William M'Dougall, and many other strong debaters, among them John Sandfield Macdonald, who had sat continuously in the Assembly since the Union—for Glengarry until the general elections of 1857, and then for Cornwall. At first he had been a Conservative, but he drifted into the Liberal ranks and remained there until after Confederation, despite periodic differences with George Brown. He opposed the Confederation movement. But we must not anticipate his career further than to say that his political attitude was at all times extremely difficult to define. That he himself would not demur to this estimate may be inferred from the fact that he was wont to describe himself, in his younger days, as a 'political Ishmaelite.' Though born and bred a Roman Catholic, he was not commonly regarded as an eminently devout member of that Church, of which he used laughingly to call himself 'an outside pillar.' The truth is that John Sandfield Macdonald was too impatient of restraint and too tenacious of his own opinions to submit to any authority. In no sense could he be called a party man.

Another member of the Opposition was the {64} young man we have already met as a student in Macdonald's law-office, afterwards Sir Oliver Mowat, prime minister of Ontario. Mowat was of a type very different to Sandfield Macdonald. He had been a consistent Reformer from his youth up. After a heated struggle, he had been elected to parliament for the South Riding of Ontario, in the general elections of 1857, over the receiver-general J. C. Morrison. On this occasion the electors were assured that the alternative presented to them was to vote for 'Mowat and the Queen' or 'Morrison and the Pope.' Mowat at once took a prominent position in the Liberal ranks, and formed one of George Brown's 'Short Administration.'

Among those who first entered parliament at the general elections of 1857 were Hector Langevin and John Rose. The former was selected to move the vote of want of confidence in the short-lived Brown-Dorion Administration. Rose at that time was a young and comparatively unknown lawyer of Montreal, in whom Macdonald had detected signs of great promise. Earlier in the same year he had accompanied Macdonald on an official mission to England. This was the beginning of a close personal friendship between the two {65} men, which lasted for more than thirty years and had no little bearing on Rose's future. On returning from England Macdonald appointed him solicitor-general for Lower Canada. In the ensuing election Rose stood for Montreal, against no less a personage than Luther H. Holton, and was elected. He was destined to fill the office of Finance minister of Canada, to become a baronet, an Imperial Privy Councillor, and a close friend of His Majesty King Edward VII, then Prince of Wales. It was believed that still higher marks of distinction were to be conferred upon him, when he died in 1888. It was said that Sir John Rose owed much of his success to the cleverness and charm of his wife. I have often heard Sir John Macdonald speak of her as a brilliant and delightful woman of the world, devoted at all times to her husband and his interests. This lady was originally Miss Charlotte Temple of Vermont. Before becoming the wife of John Rose she had been married and widowed. There had been a tragic event in her life. This was related to me by Sir John Macdonald substantially as I set it down here.

About the year 1840 there resided in Montreal a Mr and Mrs Robert Sweeny, {66} well-known and popular society people. Among the military officers stationed there was Major Henry J. Warde of the 1st Royals, a friend of the Sweenys. One day an anonymous intimation was received by Mr Sweeny to the effect that Major Warde was too attentive to his wife. Shortly afterwards the Sweenys gave a dinner, in the course of which a note, addressed to Mrs Sweeny, and a bouquet were brought in. Sweeny, whose suspicions had become thoroughly aroused, demanded to see the note. Mrs Sweeny refused, whereupon he took it from her by force. The party broke up in confusion. Sweeny rushed to the officers' mess, where Warde was dining. As he bounded up the stairs, the officers, recognizing his step, called to him to join them in a glass of wine. He entered the room, and going up to Warde then and there publicly insulted him. The inevitable duel took place next morning, and at the first shot Major Warde fell dead. Sweeny had to flee the country. He escaped to St Albans, Vermont, where he died, it was said, of remorse a few months later. What must have added poignancy to his sufferings was the statement, afterwards made, that the whole affair was a malicious plot, and that {67} the fatal missive which caused all the trouble was a forgery. Afterwards Mrs Sweeny returned to Montreal, where she went into lodgings. About the same time a raw Scottish lad, who had been teaching school in the county of Huntingdon, came to Montreal to study law. There he met Mrs Sweeny, with whom he fell in love, and they were married. This was John Rose, and Mrs Sweeny as Lady Rose lived to adorn the society of the chief Canadian cities and afterwards of London until her death in 1883.

The parliamentary record of the years immediately succeeding 1858 is not particularly interesting. George Brown continued to fight for representation by population with undiminished vigour, and although both he and his Lower-Canadian colleague, Dorion, were defeated in the general elections of 1861, he was gaining ground. The antagonism between Upper and Lower Canada yearly became more tense, and there were signs of the approach of that deadlock which was still in the future.

An agreeable occurrence of the year 1860 was the visit of the Prince of Wales to Canada. The occasion served to bring a truce to the political warfare which was being waged with {68} incredible bitterness for twelve months in the year. The Government provided for the entertainment of its royal guest and made John Rose master of the ceremonies. It is probable that out of this circumstance grew the royal friendship with which Sir John Rose was honoured in after years.

The year 1862 witnessed the defeat of the Cartier-Macdonald Government. The immediate cause was a Militia Bill. The American Civil War, and more particularly the *Trent* affair of November 1861, drew the attention of those in authority to the inadequate means of defence in Canada. In December a general order was issued calling upon the volunteer force to hold themselves in readiness for active service. The civil administration of the militia was placed in charge of Macdonald, and in January 1862 a commission was appointed with the following instructions:

1st. To report a plan for the better organization of the department of Adjutant-General of Militia.

2nd. To investigate and report upon the best means of organizing the militia, and providing an efficient and economical system for the defence of the province.

3rd. To prepare a bill or bills on the above {69} subjects, to be submitted to parliament at its next session.

The commission performed its duties with dispatch, and on April 25 Macdonald presented to parliament the fruit of its labours in the form of a bill to promote the more efficient organization of the militia of Canada. On the motion for the second reading he spoke at length concerning the reasons which made this legislation necessary. The measure had been carefully thought out, and was well adapted to the requirements of the time. It entailed, however, the expenditure of a large sum of money, and on this ground was unpopular with a certain number of Cartier's followers. On May 20 the vote on the second reading, which was taken without debate, resulted in the rejection of the bill by a majority of seven. This defeat was entirely due to defection among the Lower Canadians. Of the Upper-Canadian members the Government had a majority of seven votes.

Cartier was succeeded as prime minister by John Sandfield Macdonald, whose ally from Lower Canada was L. V. Sicotte. Sandfield Macdonald, a steadfast opponent of the proposal of representation by population, was, of course, eminently distasteful to George {70} Brown. To the Rouges this presented no difficulty. Dorion and his friends took office in the new Government. The double-majority principle was laid down as a binding rule. Its purport was that no Ministry should be held to possess the confidence of parliament unless it could command a majority from both the French and the English sections of Canada. The rule speedily proved unworkable in practice. The Macdonald-Sicotte Government was not of long duration. It had many difficulties to contend with. A reconstruction of the Cabinet in May 1863 was followed by a general election. This, however, did not improve matters for the Government. The parties in the new House were almost equally divided. The Ministry lingered on a few months, and, without waiting for a formal vote of no confidence, at last resigned on March 21, 1864.

SIR ÉTIENNE PASCAL TACHÉ

From a portrait in the John Ross Robertson Collection,
Toronto Public Library

Sir Étienne Pascal Taché.
From a portrait in the John Ross Robertson Collection,
Toronto Public Library

The Liberal-Conservatives came back to office, though not to power, under Sir Étienne Taché, who had received the honour of knighthood since last we heard of him. In less than three months his Government met defeat by a majority of two votes in the Assembly. Thus within three years four Ministries had been defeated, and two general elections had {71} failed to break the deadlock which threatened to make government impossible in Canada.

The man responsible above all others for this deplorable state of things was he who for years past had not ceased in the columns of his paper and from his place in parliament to set one section of Canada against the other; who laboured to stir up racial and religious strife; who habitually gave to the people of Upper Canada a distorted view of the national characteristics and the religious belief of their fellow-countrymen in Lower Canada. The result was that the Union formed only twenty-three years before, the Union about which such high hopes had been entertained, was on the point of breaking up. The actual *impasse* which had now been reached seems to have opened George Brown's eyes to the effects of his course, and to have convinced him that the time had arrived when a cessation of the old feuds was absolutely necessary to the carrying on of the queen's government in Canada. Impelled by a sense of patriotism and, we may well believe, at the expense of his personal feelings, he now joined hands with Macdonald and Cartier for the purpose of carrying the great scheme of Confederation. This, and this alone, promised deliverance {72} from the unhappy deadlock that impeded the progress of the country.

Since there is promised a separate account of the great work of Confederation in another volume of the present Series, I do not propose to do more here than allude to it briefly. It is known that immediately after the defeat of the Taché-Macdonald government in June 1864, Brown said to several supporters of the Administration, among them Alexander Morris and John Henry Pope, that the present crisis should be utilized to settle for ever the constitutional difficulties between Upper and Lower Canada. He assured them of his willingness to co-operate for this end. Macdonald quickly responded to the overture, and the next day he and Galt met Brown in the St Louis Hotel, Quebec. It is worthy of note that at this interview Macdonald and Galt proposed, as a remedy for existing ills, a federal union of all the British North-American provinces. Brown, on the other hand, while theoretically commending the idea, did not regard it as within the region of practical politics, but viewed its adoption as 'uncertain and remote.' His remedy was 'Parliamentary Reform, based on population, without regard to a separating line between Upper {73} and Lower Canada.' This was simply his old friend 'Representation by Population' under another name. When assured that it would be impossible to carry such a measure, Brown agreed that the Government should negotiate for a confederation of all the provinces. If this failed, they should then introduce the federal principle for Canada alone, while providing for the future incorporation of the Maritime Provinces and the North-West. On this understanding Brown, with two Reform colleagues, Oliver Mowat and William M'Dougall, entered the Cabinet. The members of the reorganized Government lost no time in applying themselves to the great object of the coalition. It so happened that, while Canadian statesmen were thus considering the question of a union of British North America, the thoughts of public men in the provinces by the Atlantic—Nova Scotia, New Brunswick, and Prince Edward Island—were turned in the direction of a union of these provinces. A convention was about to meet at Charlottetown to discuss the subject. The Canadian Government determined to take advantage of this opportunity, and eight members of the Ministry repaired to Charlottetown, where they were hospitably {74} received and were invited by the conference to express their views. They unfolded the benefits to be derived from the larger scheme with such effect that the conference agreed to adjourn and to reassemble at Quebec. The Quebec Conference met on October 10, 1864, and continued in session until the 28th of the same month. The deliberations resulted in seventy-two resolutions. These were adopted by the Canadian legislature at its next session, and formed the basis of the deliberations of the conference which assembled in the Westminster Palace Hotel, London, on December 4, 1866, under the presidency of Macdonald, for the purpose of drafting the British North America Act. These several steps, however, were not reached without the overcoming of many obstacles. The Rouge party led by Dorion was hostile to the whole project, as were Sandfield Macdonald and a few Upper-Canadian Reformers. The people of New Brunswick pronounced against the scheme at the polls before the question had been laid before their legislature. The legislature of Prince Edward Island emphatically declined a union 'which it believed would prove politically, commercially, and financially disastrous to the rights and interests of its {75} people.' George Brown quarrelled with his colleagues and left the Cabinet, which thereafter experienced a renewal of his vehement opposition.[5] Negotiations regarding reciprocity with the United States engaged the attention of the Ministry during the early part of the year 1866. Scarcely had they been disposed of when a series of Fenian attacks along the Canadian frontier caused much concern, and added largely to the cares of Macdonald, who as minister of Militia Affairs was at that time responsible for the defence of the country. His labours were incessant, his responsibility heavy, and his discouragements not a few; but with inflexible determination and rare patience he eventually surmounted all the difficulties, and on July 1, 1867, witnessed the birth of the new Dominion. From that time forth the responsibilities of his position, though greatly enlarged, were more easily borne. The sense of dependence on one province for support was no longer felt. {76} The enlargement of the arena and the inclusion of many new men of marked ability into Canadian public life tended to assuage somewhat the old-time bitterness of political strife. Perhaps more than all, the unification of the office of prime minister came as an unspeakable relief. From 1841 to 1867 the office of first minister was what might be called in commission, that is to say, there was a prime minister for each section of Canada. If an Upper Canadian were called upon to form a Ministry, his chief colleague from Lower Canada shared with him much of the authority, and also a good deal of the prestige and honour, of the office. Were a Lower Canadian summoned, his principal Upper-Canadian colleague was associated with him in the leadership of the Government. Thus Canada had the administrations of Baldwin-LaFontaine, Hincks-Morin, Taché-Macdonald, Macdonald-Cartier, Cartier-Macdonald, and others. This dual authority was perhaps necessary at the time, but it had been attended by many inconveniences, and the confederation of the provinces afforded a fitting opportunity to bring it to an end. The governor-general, Lord Monck, when confiding the duty of forming the first Dominion Cabinet to Macdonald, addressed him in these terms:

{77}

In authorizing you to undertake the duty of forming an administration for the Dominion of Canada, I desire to express my strong opinion that, in future, it shall be distinctly understood that the position of First Minister shall be held by one person, who shall be responsible to the Governor General for the appointment of the other Ministers, and that the system of dual First Ministers, which has hitherto prevailed, shall be put an end to. I think this is of importance, not only with reference to the maintenance of satisfactory relations between the Governor General and his Cabinet, but also with a view to the complete consolidation of the Union which we have brought about.[6]

On the first Dominion Day, Lord Monck announced that John A. Macdonald had been created a Knight Commander of the Bath, and that Cartier, Galt, Tilley, Tupper, Howland, and M'Dougall had been made Companions of the same order. Cartier and Galt considered this recognition of their services inadequate and declined to receive the decoration. A good deal of feeling was aroused in Lower Canada among the French {78} Canadians at what was looked upon as a slight to the representative man of their race. Cartier himself appears to have taken the matter momentarily to heart, and is said to have shown a disposition to attach some blame to Macdonald, who, of course, had nothing whatever to do with it. It was this circumstance that gave rise to the stories, echoes of which are heard even to-day, of dissensions between Macdonald and Cartier. In the first flush of his natural disappointment Cartier may have made use of some hasty expressions, and thus lent colour to a report which had no serious foundation. There never was any real breach between the two men. In order to allay the soreness, Lord Monck obtained permission to offer Cartier a baronetcy if Sir John Macdonald was agreeable. Sir John Macdonald at once replied that he would be only too glad to see his colleague thus honoured. Galt was made a K.C.M.G. at the same time, and thus the affair was brought to a happy termination. This is the whole story. It may be mentioned, as illustrating the simplicity of life during the period, that when Sir George Cartier was created a baronet, he had to borrow on his personal note the money to pay the necessary fees.

{79}

The general elections that came off shortly after the formation of the Dominion went decisively in favour of the Government — except in Nova Scotia. There it was otherwise. A violent and unreasoning opposition, led by Joseph Howe, swept all before it. Of the Conservative candidates in Nova Scotia, Sir Charles Tupper, then Dr Tupper, was the only one who carried his constituency. The remaining eighteen, including Adams Archibald, the secretary of state for the provinces, suffered defeat. It speaks not a little for Charles Tupper's influence in his native province that at the next general elections (in 1872) these figures were reversed, the Conservatives carrying twenty out of twenty-one seats. Macdonald and Tupper first met at the Confederation negotiations in 1864. They were attracted to each other at first sight, and formed an offensive and defensive alliance which was terminated only by Macdonald's death twenty-seven years later.

No single event in Sir John Macdonald's career affords a more admirable illustration of his strategic ability, delicate finesse, and subtle power over men than his negotiations with Joseph Howe. Howe's opposition to Confederation was of no ordinary kind. He {80} had long been a conspicuous figure in Nova Scotia, and was passionately devoted to the interests of the province. He was incomparably the greatest natural orator that British North America has ever produced. With the enthusiastic support of the whole province he proceeded to England, shortly after Confederation, and there, with all his great ability and eloquence, he strove for repeal. His efforts proved unavailing. Tupper was in England at the same time, not to argue the case for the Dominion, but to afford the Imperial authorities full information upon the subject. He and Howe returned on the same steamer. A few weeks later Macdonald, Cartier, and certain of their colleagues paid a visit to Halifax, where, as Macdonald naïvely records, they were received by the members of the local government with 'sufficient courtesy.' A most interesting correspondence afterwards took place between Macdonald and

Howe, with the result that early in the year 1869 Howe entered the Dominion Cabinet as president of the Privy Council. He remained there four years, and then retired to become the lieutenant-governor of Nova Scotia, in which office he died shortly afterwards.

{81}

The first session of the Dominion parliament was saddened by the assassination of Thomas D'Arcy M'Gee, one of the most gifted and charming of men, within a stone's throw of the House of Commons. An Irishman by birth, M'Gee in early life attached himself to the Young Ireland party. He took part in the insurrection of Smith O'Brien, and in consequence was obliged to flee the country. After some years spent in the United States, he settled in Montreal, where he started a newspaper. He speedily became a favourite with the Irishmen of that city, and by their influence he was returned to parliament in 1857. True to the national instinct, M'Gee began his political career as an opponent of the Government. In 1862 he accepted a portfolio under John Sandfield Macdonald, but he was dropped on the reconstruction of the Cabinet in 1863, and then passed under the influence of John A. Macdonald. The two speedily became, not merely political, but personal friends. From 1864 to 1866 they were colleagues in the Taché-Macdonald Administration. In 1865 M'Gee visited Ireland, and while there made a speech in which he unsparingly denounced Fenianism, and besought his countrymen to shun all connection with {82} that odious conspiracy. From that hour he was a marked man. M'Gee was shot from behind his back while he was entering his lodgings in Ottawa, in the early morning of April 7, 1868. Several persons were arrested for complicity in the murder. One of them, Thomas Whalen, was found guilty and was executed on February 11, 1869.

Shortly before the meeting of the first session of the first parliament of the Dominion, Sir Alexander Galt, the minister of Finance, suddenly resigned his portfolio and left the Government. His action is supposed to have been in some way connected with the failure of the Commercial Bank, which occurred about that time, but no one who knew Sir Alexander Galt would waste time in seeking to account for his actions, which often could only be accounted for by his constitutional inconstancy. In saying this I do not for a moment wish to ascribe any sordid or unworthy motive to Galt, who was a man of large and generous mind and of high honour. He was, however, never a party man. He could not be brought to understand the necessity for deferring sometimes to his leader. That spirit of subordination without which all party government becomes impossible was foreign {83} to his nature. By some impracticable persons this may be regarded as a virtue. At any rate, in Galt's case it was a fact. As Sir John Macdonald once said of him, 'Galt is as unstable as water, and never can be depended upon to be of the same mind for forty-eight hours together.'

Galt was succeeded as minister of Finance by Sir John Rose. Two years later Rose gave up his portfolio to take up residence in London as a member of the banking firm of Morton, Rose and Company. Circumstances rendered it necessary that, to maintain the arrangement entered into with Brown in 1864, Rose's successor should be an old-time Ontario Liberal, and no suitable man possessing that qualification happened to be available. But while Sir John Macdonald was casting about for a new colleague, Sir Francis Hincks reappeared on the scene. In the interval of fifteen years which had elapsed since Hincks left Canada he had been governor of various of the West India Islands, and had returned with a record of honourable service and the decoration of Knight Commander of St Michael and St George. Scarcely had Sir Francis set foot in Canada when Macdonald resolved that he should succeed Sir John Rose. {84} The offer was made and promptly accepted, and on October 9, 1869, Sir Francis Hincks was sworn of the Privy Council and appointed minister of Finance. A great storm followed. The *Globe* outdid itself in denunciation of Sir John Macdonald, of Sir Francis Hincks, and of everybody in the most remote way connected with the appointment. Richard (afterwards Sir Richard) Cartwright, hitherto a traditional Tory, took umbrage at the appointment of Hincks, and notified Sir John Macdonald no longer to count upon his support, though he did not then finally leave the Conservative party. Sir Alexander Galt also announced his withdrawal from the party, and there was dissatisfaction in other quarters. Respecting Galt's defection Sir John Macdonald wrote:

Galt came out, I am glad to say, formally in opposition and re-lieved me of the difficulty connected with him. His warm alliance with the Lower Canadian French rendered it necessary for me to put up with a good deal, as you know. But he is now finally dead as a Canadian politician. The correspondence between Cartier and himself, in which he comes squarely out {85} for independence, has rung his death-knell, and I shall take precious good care to keep him where he is. He has seduced Cartwright away, and I have found out how it was managed. Cartwright and he formed at the Club last session a sort of mutual admiration society, and they agreed that they were the two men fit to govern Canada. Galt rubbed it in pretty strong, as I have occasion to know that he told him that I ought to have selected him (Cartwright) as your succes-sor.[7]

Despite Sir John's jaunty attitude at the time, the appointment of Sir Francis Hincks could not be said to have fulfilled expectations. While it disappointed Tory ambitions, it failed to strengthen the Reform section supporting the Administration. Moreover, I infer from Sir John's confidential letters of the time that Sir Francis was not quite the square peg for the square hole.

Hincks [wrote Sir John to his friend Rose in January 1872] is as suggestive as ever in financial matters, but his rashness (always, as you know, the defect of his character) seems to increase with his years, {86} and, strange to say, he is quite a stranger to the popular opinion of Canada as it is. His Canada is the Canada of 1850. For all that he is a worthy good fellow and has been successful in finance.

Upon the whole, I am inclined to view the taking up of Sir Francis Hincks in 1869 as one of Sir John Macdonald's very few mistakes. I do not go as far as to say he would have done better to have chosen Sir Richard Cartwright, who was only thirty-three years of age at the time, and who, as the president of the Commercial Bank, which had failed only two years before, was just then an impossibility.[8] Moreover, to be quite just to Sir Richard Cartwright, I must say that

I have never seen evidence to satisfy me that he expected to succeed Sir John Rose. There is nothing in his letters preserved by Sir John Macdonald to establish this. They disclose his opposition to Hincks, but he nowhere says that he wanted {87} the position for himself. It is true that in the heat of debate Sir John more than once implied something of the kind, and I am not aware that Sir Richard ever denied the allegation, though it is quite possible he may have done so. There is little doubt, however, that the selection of Sir Francis Hincks caused Sir Richard Cartwright to abandon Sir John Macdonald. He did not leave all at once. As late as the campaign which preceded the general elections of 1872 he called himself an 'Independent,' and the *Globe* contemptuously classed him, in respect of certain votes he had given in parliament which happened to be distasteful to Brown, as 'a Tory and a corruptionist.' But from 1870 his name not infrequently appears in the division list of the House of Commons among the Opposition.

The taking over of the North-West from the Hudson's Bay Company—a troubled chapter in the early history of the Dominion—caused Sir John Macdonald a great deal of concern. Looking back after the event, it would seem that the difficulties experienced had their origin in three main causes: first, the neglect of the Hudson's Bay Company to prepare the settlers for the great change {88} involved in the transfer of the government of that vast region to Canada; secondly, the lack of conciliation, tact, and prudence on the part of the Canadian surveyors who were sent into the country in the summer of 1869; and, thirdly, the injudicious course pursued by M'Dougall, who was sent to the North-West as lieutenant-governor in anticipation of the actual transfer to Canada. The Ottawa authorities appear to have omitted no step which their scanty knowledge of that distant region might have suggested. In September 1868 a delegation, consisting of Cartier and M'Dougall, had visited England, and, after a series of untoward events and much negotiation, had arrived at an arrangement under which the Hudson's Bay Company agreed, in consideration of the sum of £300,000, to surrender all their interest in the North-West to the crown, with the reservation to the Company of one-twentieth of the fertile belt and of 45,000 acres adjacent to its trading posts. In the following September (1869) William M'Dougall was appointed lieutenant-governor, but prior to that date Joseph Howe, the secretary of state for the provinces, went to Fort Garry in order to prepare the way for the new governor. Howe found the people {89} largely uninformed as to the true position of affairs, but he added that by 'frank and courteous explanation' he had cleared the air a good deal, and that the future would depend upon M'Dougall's tact, temper, and discretion. What happened is well known — the bad handling of the situation by M'Dougall, the insurrection of the half-breeds under Louis Riel, the murder of Thomas Scott — and I shall not allude to these events further than to say that they gave Sir John Macdonald the occasion of meeting, for the first time, the future Lord Strathcona. It happened in this way. When news of the outbreak on the Red River reached Ottawa, George Stephen — between whom and Sir John Macdonald there existed a warm friendship even then — wrote to Sir John to say that he thought he knew a man well qualified to act as a peacemaker at Fort Garry if he would undertake the mission. This was Donald A. Smith, chief factor of the Hudson's Bay Company in Montreal. Armed with a letter of introduction to Macdonald from Stephen, Smith went to Ottawa. I give three brief extracts from Sir John's correspondence of the time.

I was very glad to see Mr Smith, who {90} seems a clever man; at the same time I am exceedingly disappointed at the apparent helplessness of the Hudson's Bay authorities. Mr Smith has nothing to suggest, and they seem to have been utterly neglectful at Red River of their duty in preparing the people for the change.[9]

Your friend Donald A. Smith is rather lucky. He will go up there on an important mission, will succeed beyond a doubt, and get a good deal of praise therefor.[10]

Smith left this morning with full powers and instructions. He seemed to think that he would be able to do good there. It would never have done for Colonel Wolseley to have gone with him. Smith goes to carry the olive branch, and were it known at Red River that he was accompanied by an officer high in rank in the military service, he would be looked upon as having the olive branch in one hand and a revolver in the other.[11]

{91}

Smith's mission, however, did not prove effective, and it became necessary later to send Colonel (afterwards Lord) Wolseley with a military expedition to the Red River. It may not be generally known that after the troubles were over, Colonel Wolseley intimated his willingness to accept the position of lieutenant-governor of the newly created province of Manitoba. The appointment of a military man to the civil office of lieutenant-governor was not, however, considered expedient just then, and, fortunately for the future viscount, he was passed over in favour of Adams Archibald.

Shortly after these events Sir John Macdonald, overcome by the fatigues and responsibilities of his office, fell ill, and for several months in the summer of 1870 the duties of the first minister were discharged by Sir George Cartier. Scarcely had Sir John resumed his tasks when he was appointed a member of the Joint High Commission — named to adjust all differences between Great Britain and the United States — which resulted in the Treaty of Washington, 1871. In another volume I have related,[12] mainly in his own words, the story of his strenuous fight {92} for Canadian interests on that memorable occasion. Few more interesting diplomatic memoirs were ever penned than the pages in which Macdonald recounts from day to day his efforts to discharge his duties to the Empire as Her Majesty's plenipotentiary, and at the same time to protect and defend the special interests of Canada. That he upheld Imperial interests was never questioned, but he was accused by some of his political opponents at the time of having done so at the expense of Canada. It was alleged that he had sacrificed the fisheries to enable Her Majesty's government to come to terms with the United States. In this, as in many other matters, time has amply vindicated his course.

The treaty — in regard to which he had apprehensions — received the sanction of the Canadian House of Commons by a vote of more than two to one. At the ensuing general election the province of Nova Scotia — the home of Canadian fishermen — ratified Macdonald's policy by returning twenty members out of twenty-one in its support. It is clear that he had not sacrificed Canadian interests, for when the Fishery Articles were terminated in 1885, it was not by desire of {93} Great Britain or of Canada, but by the action of the United States.

The summer of 1871 was marked by the admission of British Columbia into the Confederation. By the terms of this union Canada was pledged to construct a railway to the Pacific within ten years. This was strenuously objected to by the parliamentary Opposition. It was an obligation, the Liberals said, that would press with crushing severity upon the people of Canada. They argued that in contracting to build the road in ten years the Government had committed Canada to an undertaking greatly beyond its resources; indeed, to a physical impossibility.

In December of the same year the Government in Ontario led by Sandfield Macdonald was defeated in the legislature and compelled to resign. An Administration, determinedly hostile to the Ottawa Government, was formed at Toronto under Edward Blake. The Ontario Orangemen were filled with anger at the brutal murder of Thomas Scott by Louis Riel at Fort Garry and the failure of the Government at Ottawa to seize the murderer. The anti-confederate feeling was still strong in Nova Scotia. There was dissatisfaction over the appointment of Sir Francis Hincks. {94} In many quarters the Washington Treaty was unpopular. All this hostility Macdonald had to face, as well as the strenuous opposition of the Liberal party. It was under these untoward circumstances that Sir John Macdonald advised the dissolution of the House of Commons and appealed to the people in the summer of 1872. His feelings on the eve of the battle are thus expressed in a letter to Sir John Rose:

I am, as you may fancy, exceedingly desirous of carrying the election again; not with any personal object, because I am weary of the whole thing, but Confederation is only yet in the gristle, and it will require five years more before it hardens into bone.

It is only by the exercise of constant prudence and moderation that we have been able to prevent the discordant elements from ending in a blow-up. If good Constitutional men are returned, I think that at the end of five years the Dominion may be considered safe from being prejudiced by any internal dissension.[13]

{95} The fight in Ontario proved very severe, as may be gathered from his subsequent account:

I had to fight a stern and up-hill battle in Ontario, and had I not taken regularly to the stump, a thing that I have never done before, we should have been completely routed. The chief ground of attack on the Government was the Washington Treaty, and our submitting to Gladstone's resolve not to press the Fenian claims. Added to this, of course, were all the sins of omission and commission that gather round an administration of so many years' duration as ours.

I never worked so hard before, and never shall do so again; but I felt it to be necessary this time. I did not want a verdict against the treaty from the country, and besides, I sincerely believe that the advent of the Opposition, as it is now constituted, to power would greatly damage the future of Confederation. That Opposition has much deteriorated since you left Canada. Poor Sandfield is gone; Brown is out of public life, or rather out of Parliament; Blake, who is a gentleman by birth and education, has broken down in health; {96} Dorion has all but retired from public life, and was elected against his will and in his absence; and the rest, with one or two exceptions, are a very inferior lot.[14]

In spite of Sir John's efforts the Government lost ground heavily. Sir Francis Hincks suffered defeat in South Brant, and Sir George Cartier in East Montreal. What Sir Richard Cartwright used to call 'the shreds and patches of the Dominion'—the Maritime Provinces and British Columbia—did very well for the Conservatives, but, taking it altogether, it was plain that the Government had sustained a severe check.

Sir John A. Macdonald in 1872

The Opposition, alive to their improved chances, assembled in full force at the session of 1873, under the leadership of Alexander

Mackenzie. In order to render more effective service to his party at Ottawa, Edward Blake resigned office as prime minister of Ontario in favour of Oliver Mowat. All along he had held a seat in the House of Commons, for those were days of dual representation, when there was nothing to prevent a man from sitting in both a provincial House and the House of Commons. This several leading men did. {97} It will be readily understood, however, that the office of prime minister of Ontario would materially interfere with the duties of a leading member of the Opposition at Ottawa. With large reinforcements and a feeling of confidence, the Opposition gathered for the fray, determined, if possible, to compass the overthrow of the Macdonald Government. Fortune favoured the design, for in the session of 1873 occurred what has come to be commonly known as the 'Pacific Scandal.'

Briefly stated, the charge involved in the Pacific Scandal was this: that the Government had corruptly granted to Sir Hugh Allan and his associates the charter for the building of the Canadian Pacific Railway, in consideration of a large sum of money supplied by him for election purposes. In a letter addressed to Lord Dufferin, which has been before the public for twenty years, Sir John Macdonald completely answered this accusation.[15]

{98}

In the light of all that has happened in the last forty years, it is difficult to repress a smile when reading the impassioned invectives poured out upon Sir John Macdonald by his political opponents of that day in connection with the Pacific Scandal. According to them he had basely betrayed his country, selling her honour for filthy lucre; he had shamefully prostituted his office; he was a great criminal for whose punishment justice cried aloud, and much more to the same effect. Yet every one who dispassionately considers the affair to-day in its true perspective sees quite plainly that, however indiscreetly he acted in his {99} relations with Sir Hugh Allan, Sir John's sole thought was for the advantage of Canada. In the face of great difficulties he had carried Confederation, had pacified Nova Scotia, had brought Manitoba, British Columbia, and Prince Edward Island into the Union; and in order that this Union should abide, he was putting forth all his energies for the construction of the great link that was to hold the distant provinces together.

In all these matters he had to encounter at every step the rancorous opposition of his political adversaries. It is, therefore, not surprising that he attached much importance to the general elections of 1872. He had no personal ambitions unfulfilled—he was weary of it all—but he entertained a profound {100} conviction that to confide the destinies of Canada to men who, among other things, were opposing the building of the Canadian Pacific Railway by every means in their power, would be to undo the great work to which he had set his hand and to disrupt the Confederation. 'With five years more,' he writes, 'I thought we might safely consider that the gristle had hardened into bone, and that the Union had been thoroughly cemented.' And so we find him, though far from strong, throwing himself with vigour into the elections of 1872, and, his colleagues being everywhere hard pressed, himself doing much that might better have been confided to others. Every one knows, to use the expression of the late Israel Tarte, that 'elections are not made with prayers.' Every one knows, and it is mere hypocrisy to disclaim the knowledge, that there are election funds in both parties, to which wealthy friends of the respective parties are invited to contribute. Sir John's mistake was in asking favours of a man who at that time was seeking advantages from the Government. No matter how sure he might be of his own rectitude, it was setting a dangerous precedent for a weaker man, who might be placed in his position, to follow. No doubt, too, he would have {101} done better not to have mixed himself up with money matters at all, though in acting as he did he only followed the usual practice. In that day the leaders of political parties in Canada personally solicited campaign funds.[16] Macdonald took contributions from the rich men of his party— among others from Sir Hugh Allan—to fight that party's battles. But there was no barter. Sir Hugh Allan was, of course, playing his own game. His motive is quite apparent. He wanted to build the Pacific Railway, and was naturally interested in preventing the accession to power of men opposed to the whole scheme as premature and beyond the resources of the country.

What seems plain now was not so apparent forty years ago. The current set in strongly {102} against the Ministry. As Mr S. H. Blake would say, 'There was the sound of a going in the tops of the mulberry trees.' There was a general feeling that the days of the Government were numbered. The country was ripe for a change. The Conservatives had been in office for nearly ten years consecutively, and people were beginning to get a little tired of them. Men began to think that it was time to give the other side a chance. Long periods of exclusion from office of the representatives of nearly one-half the community is not good for the Opposition, for the state, nor for the dominant party itself. Sir John Macdonald, at a later period, seems to have recognized this, for one of his letters, written to a friend on the eve of the contest of 1887, contains the significant words, 'the Government is too old.' It was not as old as was his Government at its resignation in 1873. However that may be, amid shrieks of 'corruption' the Administration of Sir John Macdonald bowed to public opinion, and the Liberals at last got their chance.

In the general elections, which took place in the month of January 1874, the newly formed Mackenzie Government swept the country, returning with a majority of {103} seventy-five or upwards. Among the new members was Mr (now Sir Wilfrid) Laurier.

Alexander Mackenzie, the prime minister, like his predecessor, was a Scotsman by birth. Like Sir John Macdonald, too, he had emigrated to Canada at an early age and had settled first at Kingston, subsequently removing to Sarnia. In 1861 he entered parliament as member for Lambton, and took rank from the first as a strong and effective debater on the side of the Opposition. In office he proved a capable administrator of unimpeachable integrity, with a remarkable capacity for labour. It could not be said of him, however, that he possessed the essential qualities of a leader. Not only was he destitute of that mysterious personal attribute known as 'magnetism,' but he was disposed to be arbitrary and dictatorial. His political supporters respected and perhaps feared him, but it cannot be said that he was popular among them.

Goldwin Smith was once driving a newly arrived English friend through the streets of Toronto at the time Mackenzie was in the zenith of his power. When passing Mackenzie's house he remarked the fact. 'And who is Mr Mackenzie?' inquired the {104} friend. 'Mr

Mackenzie,' replied Goldwin Smith, 'was a stonemason; *he is a stonemason still.*'

This, of course, was not fair. Mackenzie, despite his narrowness, rigidity, faults of manner, and perhaps of temper, was an able man. No fairer was Goldwin Smith's cynical observation that the alliance between Macdonald and Brown in 1864 was 'as brief and perfidious as a harlot's love'; but nobody—at any rate, no Canadian public man—ever looked for fairness from Goldwin Smith, whose idea of independence seemed to consist of being alternately unjust to each side. Both sayings, however, are extremely clever, and both had sufficient truth about them to give point at once to the author's malevolence and to his wit.

A man of very different mould from that of the Liberal leader was his nominal follower Edward Blake, one of the rarest minds that have adorned the bar of Canada or of any other country. Blake was not merely a great equity lawyer; he was, as well, a distinguished authority on the principles of government. Viewed as intellectual performances, his speeches in the Canadian House of Commons have never been surpassed. But to his great {105} gifts were joined great weaknesses, among which may be set down an abnormal sensitiveness. He was peculiarly susceptible to the daily annoyances which beset a public man. So marked was this infirmity that men without a tithe of his ability, but with a better adjusted nervous system, would sometimes presume to torment him just for the fun of the thing. While he was minister of Justice, political exigencies compelled Mackenzie to take into his Cabinet a man who, by reason of his unsavoury political record, was eminently distasteful to Blake. This man knew perfectly well that the great lawyer was not proud of the association, but being as thick-skinned as Blake was sensitive, he rather enjoyed his colleague's discomfort. He was known to go into Blake's office on a short winter's afternoon, and, standing with his back to the fire in a free and easy attitude as though perfectly at home, to say, 'Well, *mon cher collègue*' (here Blake would visibly writhe, to the equally apparent delight of the intruder), 'I have called for you to come for a walk with me.' 'My good sir,' Blake would tartly reply, 'I have work here that will keep me for the next two hours.' 'But it will be dark then,' objected the caller. 'Well, my good {106} sir,' was the retort, 'we can walk in the dark, I suppose'—which Blake would naturally much prefer. Edward Blake's outward bearing was cold and unsympathetic. He was often repellent to those desiring to be his friends. Intimates he appeared to have none: he would not allow people to be intimate with him. He would hardly even, when leader of the Opposition, accept the co-operation of his supporters or allow them a share in his labours. So exacting was his standard that he felt no one would do the work as well as himself, and any one who proffered assistance was likely to get a snub for his pains. Whenever he spoke in the House of Commons, he so exhausted his subject that there was nothing left for his followers to say—an impolitic course for a leader. Yet it was impossible, such is the compelling power of genius, to withhold admiration for that lonely and impressive figure whose external bearing spoke so plainly of the intellectual force within. I had the honour of only a slight personal acquaintance with Blake, yet I never recall his memory without a tinge of sadness that so gifted a man should not have accomplished more in the way of constructive statesmanship. Before the age of forty he was prime minister of {107} Ontario, but within a twelvemonth he gave it up to devote his attention to federal politics. When the Liberal party succeeded to power in 1873, men thought that Blake's opportunity had at last arrived, and it was learned with surprise that he had not taken a portfolio in the new Administration. He had, however, a seat in the Cabinet, but this he resigned within three months. In 1875 he re-entered the Cabinet as minister of Justice. But, beyond writing a few masterly dispatches on the pardoning power and obtaining certain modifications in the governor-general's instructions in that regard, he does not appear to have accomplished much during his tenure of office. The bill establishing the Supreme Court, passed about this time, was the work primarily of Sir John Macdonald, and was piloted through the House of Commons by Telesphore Fournier, Blake's immediate predecessor in the department of Justice. Early in 1878 Blake again left the Cabinet, and he was not even in the country during the elections of that year which overwhelmed his late colleagues. He became leader of the Opposition after the retirement of Mackenzie in 1880, but resigned the post after his failure to carry the elections of 1887. He afterwards {108} went to Great Britain, and became a Nationalist member from Ireland of the House of Commons. For fifteen years his great talents lay obscured at Westminster in the shadows of Parnell and Redmond. Broken in health, he finally returned to his native country; but it was only to die.

But if Blake's mind was not of the constructive order, his critical and analytical faculties were highly developed. Always effective, often trenchant, sometimes cruel, his powers of sarcasm and invective were unrivalled. Once, when a former minister of Inland Revenue, not remarkable for his knowledge of the affairs of his department, had proposed a resolution to the effect that a barrel should no longer be considered a measure of capacity, Blake offered an amendment to the effect that 'in future the office of Cabinet minister be no longer considered a measure of capacity!' Again, in one of his orations against the building of the Canadian Pacific Railway, he prefaced a minute and exhaustive narration of events connected with the enterprise in these words: 'Mr Speaker, on the first of April—*a fitting day*—in the year 1871, ...' That was his estimate of the project as late as the early eighties.

{109}

During Blake's period of office an old and faithful official of his department, who rather prided himself upon his discrimination in the use of words, wrote on a file of papers, 'Referred to the Minister for his instructions.' When this came before Blake, he wrote underneath the memorandum: 'My officers do not *refer* matters to me; they *submit* them.—E.B.' It is due to Blake to say that, when leaving the department, he called for this file and expunged these words with his own hand.

Sometimes, however, he was in lighter vein, and, indeed, I have known him to betray a transient gleam of humour. One day a letter, the envelope addressed to Blake, was left at 'Earnscliffe,' Macdonald's Ottawa residence. The letter inside, however, as appeared later, was addressed to Sir John Macdonald. Ignorant, of course, of this fact, Macdonald sent it to Blake, who returned it with this note:

COBOURG, *June 28th*, 1889.

MY DEAR SIR,—Thanks for the mysterious package, which, however, I return, perceiving that in this, as in some other cases, if I have a better title to the shell, you have the better title to the oyster.

It is a curious example of the workings {110} of the mind and of the phraseology of a deaf mute. It is a sad sort of letter, and I intend to write to Jones to enquire if anything can be done for the poor creature.

Yours faithfully,
EDWARD BLAKE.

Here we get a glimpse of the really kind and generous heart that beat under the chilling exterior of Edward Blake.

In the year 1875 there occurred in Montreal an event which caused a good deal of ill-feeling between the English and French sections of the population throughout the province of Quebec. This was the epilogue of the famous Guibord case. Joseph Guibord was a member of a society known as *L'Institut Canadien*. In 1858 the Roman Catholic bishop of Montreal issued a pastoral letter exhorting the members of this institute to purge their library of certain works regarded as immoral, and decreeing several penalties, including deprivation of the sacraments and refusal of ecclesiastical burial, in the event of disobedience. The library committee returned a reply to the effect that they were the judges of the morality of their books, and, further, that there were no immoral works in their library. {111} The matter appears to have lain dormant for some years. In 1865 several members of the Institute, including Guibord, appealed to Rome against the action of the bishop, but in vain. Shortly afterwards Guibord died, and as he had adhered to his membership in the Institute despite the bishop's *mandement*, ecclesiastical burial was refused. His widow had recourse to the law, and ultimately the Judicial Committee of the Privy Council ordered the burial of Guibord's remains in the Roman Catholic cemetery. The reasons upon which this judgment is based are that the Church of Rome in the province of Quebec, while lacking some of the features of an established church, differs materially before the law from voluntary religious bodies; that certain privileges, such as the right to collect tithes, secured to it by law, beget corresponding obligations towards the laity. One obligation is to give ecclesiastical sepulchre to its members. The proceedings against Guibord had been legally insufficient to deprive him of this right; he had not been excommunicated personally and by name, but merely lay under a general excommunication.

The first attempts of Guibord's friends to bury the body in accordance with this {112} decision were frustrated by force; but on November 16, 1875, under a strong military escort, the remains of Joseph Guibord were finally laid to rest in the Côte des Neiges cemetery, in the presence of a sullen assemblage. This forcible, albeit legal, proceeding was deeply felt by many who needed not to take lessons in loyalty to the Queen from the members of the Institut Canadien, but who could not see why the Church of Rome should be debarred the right, supposed to appertain to every society, of determining its own conditions of membership, nor understand why the friends of a man should seek on his behalf, after his death, the ministrations of that Church whose teachings, during his lifetime, he had voluntarily despised.

The Liberal Government came to power in 1873 at a time of commercial depression extending over the whole continent. Canada suffered severely; and so did the Ministry. Business was bad, the revenues fell off, employment became scarce. It was during this period that the Conservative Opposition began the advocacy of what was called 'The National Policy'—a system of modified protection which it was hoped would both stimulate the industries of the country and {113} provide a sufficient revenue. Protection was no new policy with Sir John Macdonald. As long before as in 1846 he had advocated it from his place in parliament. In 1850 he belonged to an association which had as one of its aims a 'commercial national policy.' In 1858 he was joint-leader of a Government whose finance minister (Galt) announced protection to native industries as its policy. In 1861 he at various times and places expounded and developed this policy. Lastly, on the eve of the general elections of 1872, he wrote to the present Lord Mount Stephen:

At the hustings in Western Canada [Ontario] and in all the constituencies except Toronto, the battle will be between free trade and a national policy.... It is really astonishing the feeling that has grown up in the West [he is referring to Western Ontario] in favour of encouragement of home manufactures.

In 1876 the time was opportune for promoting this policy. Trade was depressed, manufactures languished, and the Canadian people as producers only of raw material were fast becoming hewers of wood and drawers of water for their more opulent neighbours in {114} the United States. On March 10 of that year Sir John Macdonald propounded to the House of Commons his scheme for improving the commerce of the country. His proposals were contemptuously received by the Government. The prime minister, while admitting the serious character of the depression then prevailing, attributed the cause wholly to circumstances beyond their control, and denied the power of any government to remove it by legislation. They would have nothing to do with protection, which Mackenzie ridiculed as an attempt to relieve distress by imposing additional taxation.

Sir John thought differently. If he had done nothing else, his 'National Policy' campaign would have stamped him as a leader of men. In the words of a political opponent of the time, 'he constructed with consummate skill the engine which destroyed the Mackenzie Administration. From the very first he saw what a tactician would do with Protection, and in so masterly a manner did he cover his troops with that rampart, that it was impossible for the Liberals to turn their flank.'

His political picnics in 1876 and 1877, and the enthusiasm he everywhere aroused, were long remembered, and are not forgotten to {115} this day by older men. Everywhere crowds gathered to his support, and the country impatiently waited the opportunity to restore him to his old position at the head of affairs. At length the fateful day arrived, and on September 17, 1878, the people of Canada declared by an overwhelming majority for 'John A.' and protection. In the preceding July Sir John had ventured a prophecy of the result—something, by the way, he was extremely chary of doing. 'If we do well we shall have a majority of sixty, if badly, thirty.' He had eighty-six.

It was observed that as far as possible the new ministers in the Cabinet formed by Macdonald were taken from the ranks of his old colleagues, from those who had suffered with him on account of the

'Pacific Scandal.' Sir George Cartier was dead, but Tilley and Tupper, Langevin, Pope, Campbell, Aikins, O'Connor, and others of the 'Old Guard' not hitherto of Cabinet rank, became members of the new Administration, which was destined to last for thirteen years.

Lord Dufferin's term of office as governor-general was about to expire. One of his last acts before leaving Canada was to send for Macdonald to form the new Ministry. Sir {116} John's relations with Lord Dufferin had always been pleasant, though I think he considered the governor-general a bit of a humbug. Speaking to me one day of men's liking for flattery, Sir John said that 'almost anybody will take almost any amount of it,' but he thought that Lord Dufferin transgressed even those wide limits. 'He laid it on with a trowel.' Sir John added that Lord Dufferin was proud of his classical acquirements. He once delivered an address in Greek at the University of Toronto. A newspaper subsequently spoke of 'His Excellency's perfect command of the language.' 'I wonder who told the reporter that,' said a colleague to the chief. 'I did,' replied Sir John. 'But you do not know Greek.' 'No,' replied Sir John, 'but I know men.'

Lord Dufferin's successor in the office of governor-general was the Duke of Argyll, at that time Marquess of Lorne, who spent five interesting and, as the duke himself said more than once, pleasant years in the Dominion. The personal relations between him and the prime minister were always of the most agreeable description. The story, published in Sir Richard Cartwright's *Reminiscences*, that Sir John Macdonald was guilty on one occasion {117} of rudeness to his royal consort the Princess Louise is without a particle of foundation. It was categorically denied by Her Royal Highness, and characterized as 'rubbish' by the duke in a cable to the Montreal *Star*. I have now arrived at the stage in this narrative when I have personal knowledge of everything upon which I write. I was Sir John Macdonald's private secretary during the latter half of Lord Lorne's term of office, and I positively assert that the relations between Government House and Earnscliffe were of the most friendly character during the whole period. Had there been the slightest truth in the story, it is incredible that such relations should have existed.

The policy of protection which Sir John had offered to the people in 1878 was brought into effect during the session of 1879. So completely was his promise fulfilled that the Liberal leader, Mackenzie, declared that Sir John had 'gone the whole hog.' George Brown made a similar admission.[17] Sir John Macdonald, it may be said, always carried out his promises. I never knew him to fail. He was guarded in making them, but if he gave an unconditional promise he was sure to {118} implement it, no matter at what inconvenience to himself. I have seen this illustrated again and again. The late Sir Richard Cartwright—no very friendly witness—observed in recent times, in his own characteristic fashion: 'I will say this for that old scoundrel John A. Macdonald, that if he once gave you his word, you could rely upon it.'

Sir John had not been long in power when death removed the most implacable of his foes. On May 9, 1880, died George Brown, struck down in his office by the bullet of an assassin. This shocking occurrence, which was due to the act of a discharged printer, had no relation to public affairs.

The fiscal policy having been settled, Sir John Macdonald again turned his attention to the problem of a railway to the Pacific. The Liberal Government, on the ground that the agreement with British Columbia to build the road within ten years was impossible of fulfilment, had not considered Canada bound by it, but had decided to build the railway, not by means of a private company, but as a government work, and to construct it gradually in sections as the progress of settlement and the state of the public treasury might warrant. Sir John Macdonald rejected this piecemeal {119} policy, and resolved to carry out the original scheme of a great national highway across the continent, to be built as rapidly as possible so as to open up quickly the resources of the Great West.

In the summer of 1880, accompanied by three of his colleagues— Tupper, Pope, and Macpherson—Macdonald visited England for the purpose of inducing capitalists to take hold of the enterprise. After much negotiation they were successful, and on September 14, 1880, an agreement for the construction of the Canadian Pacific Railway was signed in London. The company was to receive $25,000,000 and 25,000,000 acres of land in alternate blocks on each side of the railway running from Winnipeg to Jasper House at the Rockies. The line was to be completed by May 1, 1891, and the company was to deposit one million dollars as evidencing its ability to carry out the bargain. The contract was finally executed at Ottawa on October 21, 1880. Parliament was then summoned in order to ratify what the Government had done.

The contract was fiercely opposed. The Opposition denounced the terms as extravagant, as beyond the resources of the country, {120} and as certain to involve financial disaster. Blake affirmed that the road would never pay for the grease for the wheels of the engines that would pass over it, and appealed to his fellow-members not to throw the hard-earned money of the people of Canada 'down the gorges of British Columbia.' A rival company was hurriedly got up which offered to build the railway on much more moderate terms. The *bona fides* of this opposition company or 'syndicate' was much doubted, and, in any event, the proposal came too late. The Government was bound to stand by its bargain, which was defended with great power by Sir John Macdonald, Sir Charles Tupper, and others. At length, by a vote of 128 to 49, the House of Commons ratified the contract, which passed the Senate a few days later, and became incorporated in an Act of Parliament assented to on February 15, 1881.

Then began a period of railway construction hitherto unparalleled. At the date of the signing of the contract the only portions of the main line built were 152 miles from Fort William westward (the track was laid, but the line was not completed) and 112 miles from Keewatin to Selkirk—that is 264 miles. Mackenzie had declared the building of the road {121} within ten years to be a physical impossibility for Canada. He even went so far as to affirm that the whole resources of the British Empire could not construct the railway in ten years.[18] As a matter of fact, it was built by Canada in less than five years. On November 7, 1885, Donald Smith drove the last spike at Craigellachie, twenty-eight miles west of Revelstoke, British Columbia; and on the 24th of the following July, just fifteen years (including the five lost years of the Mackenzie régime) after the engagement with British Columbia was made, Sir John Macdonald {122} arrived at Port Moody in the car in which he had left Ottawa a few days before.

This marvellous feat was not accomplished without great exertions, much anxiety, and the exercise of the highest arts of statesmanship. The opposition to the granting of the charter had been so keen, the arguments against the whole scheme had been so powerfully set forth, that the company found they could not sell their lands, nor obtain, in any other way, the money needed to carry forward the work. The Government was obliged to come to the rescue, and, in the session of 1884, to grant a loan of $22,500,000 to the company. On December 1, 1883, Sir John Macdonald sent this telegram to Sir Charles Tupper, who only a few months before had gone over to London to fill the position of high commissioner: 'Pacific in trouble, you should be here.' Next morning the characteristic reply was received: 'Sailing on Thursday.' Sir Charles was as good as his word. With admirable courage, energy, and resolution he fought the measure of relief through parliament, and for a time at least all was well. But only for a time. Early in the year 1885 we find Mr Stephen, the president of the company, writing Sir John Macdonald:

{123}

There is imminent danger of sudden crisis unless we can find means to meet pressing demands.... It is clear as noon-day, Sir John, that unless you yourself say what is to be done, nothing but disaster will result. The question is too big for some of our friends, and nothing but your own authority and influence can carry anything that will accomplish the object.... I endeavoured to impress upon him again [the finance minister] that the object of the present application to the Government is to save the *life* of the Company....

I do hope something will be done to-day that will have the effect of saving the life of the Company. I stayed over here [Ottawa] to-day in case I might be wanted. It is impossible for me to carry on this struggle for life, in which I have now been for over four months constantly engaged, any longer. Although I have done my best to save the life and the honour of the Company, I cannot help feeling that I have failed to impress the Government with a full sense of the extreme urgency of the necessities of the Company, and yet I do not know anything further that I can say {124} or do to enable the Government to realize the extreme gravity of the position in which the Company is now placed. If the Company is allowed once to go to the wall, the remedial measures proposed will be useless because too late. I shall be within reach if wanted. Mr Pope, your secretary, knows where to find me.

The following is part of a telegram from the general manager to the president:

Have no means paying wages, pay car can't be sent out, and unless we get immediate relief we must stop. Please inform Premier and Finance Minister. Do not be surprised, or blame me, if an immediate and most serious catastrophe happens.

The application referred to was for a further loan of $5,000,000. The request was ill received by the Cabinet. Ministers were decidedly averse to any further assistance out of the public treasury. The prime minister was told that it could not be done. On the other hand, if it were not done, irretrievable disaster stared Canada in the face. For if the Canadian Pacific Railway went down, what of the future of the North-West? what of the credit {125} of Canada itself? This was perhaps the supreme moment of Sir John Macdonald's career. With a divided Cabinet, an unwilling following, and a hostile Opposition, it is no wonder that even his iron resolution shrank from going to parliament with this fresh proposal, which seemed an absolute confirmation of the prophecies of his opponents. He had, I believe, almost if not altogether, made up his mind that further assistance was impossible. But he looked once again, and appreciated the herculean efforts that his friends George Stephen and Donald Smith were making to avert the ruin of the great enterprise, apparently tottering to its fall. He realized what such a fall would mean to his country, to his party, and to himself; and, summoning all his courage, he called a final Cabinet council and placed the issue fully before his colleagues. The master spirit prevailed.[19] One minister withdrew his resignation, and he with other {126} ministers abandoned their opposition. The ministerial supporters in parliament, cheered and encouraged by the indomitable spirit of their chief, voted the $5,000,000, and the road was carried forward to completion. From that day all went well. Both loans were speedily repaid by the company; and the Canadian Pacific Railway, to-day the greatest transportation system in the world, was launched.

It is the infelicity of statesmen that one difficulty is no sooner overcome than another arises to take its place. And so it now happened. In 1885 Louis Riel led an armed rebellion of half-breeds on the banks of the Saskatchewan, as fifteen years earlier he had led one on the banks of the Red River. The causes were similar. The half-breeds were alarmed at the incoming of new life, and could not get from the Government a title to the lands they occupied that they regarded as secure. The rebellion was quickly crushed and Riel was taken prisoner. This opened up a fresh chapter of embarrassments for the Ministry. From the first there could be no doubt as to the course which should be pursued with regard to the unfortunate man. His offences of fifteen years before had been suffered to pass into oblivion. Even his great {127} crime—the atrocious murder of Thomas Scott—had gone unwhipped of justice. His subsequent effrontery in offering himself for election and attempting to take his seat in parliament had been visited with no greater punishment than expulsion from the House of Commons. Now he had suddenly emerged from his obscurity in the United States to lead the half-breeds along the Saskatchewan river in an armed revolt against the Government. At the same time—and this was incomparably his worst offence—he had deliberately incited the Indians to murder and pillage. He had caused much bloodshed, the expenditure of large sums of money, and the disturbance of an extensive region of the North-West.

Riel had been caught red-handed. Whatever excuses might be put forward, on behalf of his unfortunate dupes, that the Government had refused to heed their just demands, it is certain that Riel himself could plead no such excuses, for he was not at the time even a resident of the country. But, unfortunately, his case gave the opportunity of making political capital against the Government. Since he was of French origin the way was open for an appeal to racial passions. The French-Canadian habitant, {128} recalling the rebellion of 1837-38, saw in Riel another Papineau. A wretched malefactor, thus elevated to the rank of a patriot, became a martyr in the eyes of many of his compatriots. Sir John Macdonald fully realized the danger of the situation, but from the first he was resolved, whatever the political outcome, that if proved a culprit Riel should not a second time escape. There should be a fair trial and no more clemency, but rigorous justice, for the man who had added new crimes to the murder of Scott fifteen years earlier. Four able lawyers, including Sir Charles Fitzpatrick, the present chief justice of Canada, were assigned to Riel's defence. The trial opened at Regina on July 20, 1885, and on August 1 Riel was found guilty of high treason and sentenced to be hanged on September 18. In deference to those who professed to doubt Riel's sanity, a stay of execution was granted. Sir John Macdonald sent to Regina two medical men, who, with the surgeon of the North-West Mounted Police, were instructed to examine into Riel's mental condition. They reported that, except in regard to certain religious matters on which he appeared to hold eccentric and foolish views, he was quite able to distinguish between right and wrong and that he {129} was entirely responsible for his actions. On November 16, 1885, Riel paid upon the scaffold the last penalty for his crimes.

During Riel's imprisonment Sir John Macdonald received from him several letters. From various other quarters he was informed of the blasphemies, outrages, and murders of which Riel had been guilty. There were many petitions, some for justice, others for mercy, chiefly from people living in the eastern provinces. These, however, counted for little, since for the most part they merely represented the political or racial sympathies of the writers. But there are among Macdonald's papers some original statements in respect to Riel of the highest importance, from those of his fellow-countrymen who best knew him. The Catholic missionaries living in the districts specially affected by the rebellion—St Laurent, Batoche, and Duck Lake—in a collective letter dated March 12, 1885, denounced in the strongest language 'the miscreant Louis David Riel' who had led astray their people. The venerable bishop of St Albert, while pleading for Riel's dupes, had no word of pity for the 'miserable individual' himself. Under date July 11, 1885, the bishop writes thus to Sir John Macdonald:

{130}

These poor halfbreeds would never have taken up arms against the Government had not a miscreant of their own nation [Riel], profiting by their discontent, excited them thereto. He gained their confidence by a false and hypocritical piety, and having drawn them from the beneficent influence of their clergy, he brought them to look upon himself as a prophet, a man inspired by God and specially charged with a mission in their favour, and forced them to take up arms.

Riel's own letters disclose no appreciation on his part of the enormity of his offences, or of the grave peril in which he stood. The whole collection produces a most unfavourable impression of the man, and one rises from its examination with a wish that those who were wont to proclaim Riel a patriot and hero could see for themselves what manner of man he really was. The papers will ultimately find their resting-place in the Dominion Archives and will become available to future historians.

The political effect of the execution of Riel was quite in accordance with Sir John Macdonald's expectations. In the province of Quebec the greatest excitement prevailed. {131} At many meetings the prime minister and his French Canadian colleagues were burned in effigy. Sir John had postponed an intended visit to England until after the execution. So intense was the popular feeling, that when the time came for sailing he thought it prudent to avoid Montreal and Quebec and to board his ship at Rimouski. This circumstance afforded material to the editor of the *Mail*, Mr Edward Farrer, for an amusing article, bearing the alliterative title, 'The Murderer's Midnight Mizzle, or the Ruffian's Race for Rimouski.'

All this happened in November. In the preceding January Sir John had taken part at Montreal in a magnificent demonstration to celebrate the fortieth anniversary of his entrance into public life. If ever a public man enjoyed the acclaim of the populace, the Conservative chieftain did so on that occasion. If my memory serves me rightly, the crowd took the horses out of his carriage and drew him in triumph from the place of meeting to his hotel. Not quite ten months later, when slipping almost secretly past Montreal, Macdonald alluded to this as an apt illustration of the fickleness of public opinion. The immediate consequence of this popular frenzy in Quebec was the defeat of the Conservative {132} Government of the province, the rise of Honoré Mercier, the Liberal leader, to power, and the loss of many Conservative seats in the subsequent Dominion elections. Indeed, Sir John Macdonald never recovered his ground in the province of Quebec. Riel's execution wrought organic political changes which are visible to this day.

The parliamentary opponents of the Government were naturally not slow to take advantage of the situation, but their first move was frustrated by Sir John Macdonald in a manner worthy to rank as a piece of political strategy with the 'Double Shuffle' itself. At the first available moment after the meeting of parliament in February 1886, the member for Montmagny[20] moved this resolution: 'That this House feels it its duty to express its deep regret that the sentence of death passed upon Louis Riel convicted of high treason was allowed to be carried into execution.' Scarcely were the words out of his mouth before Sir Hector Langevin rose, anticipating Blake, the leader of the Opposition, by a fraction of a second, and moved the 'previous question,' {133} thus shutting off all amendments, and compelling a vote to be taken on the resolution as it stood. The Opposition had naturally counted upon having an opportunity to present an amendment so framed as to censure the Government for maladministration, without categorically condemning the execution itself. In this design, however, they were frustrated. Blake was completely outgeneralled, and as Sir Hector had been fortunate enough to catch the speaker's eye first, there was no help for it. Blake himself, his French-Canadian supporters, and some others, voted for the condemnation of the Government, but for some of the most prominent members of the Opposition this was an impossibility. Many prominent Liberals—including Mackenzie, Cartwright, Mulock, Paterson, Sutherland, Fisher, and Davies—supported the Ministry against their own leader. By a vote of 146 to 52 the House rejected Landry's motion.

Another important question of the time was the adoption of an Act for the Dominion making a uniform qualification of voters. The British North America Act laid down that, until the parliament of

Canada otherwise provided, the provincial laws relating to the qualification to vote at elections should apply {134} to elections for members of the House of Commons. Since 1867 parliament had gone on using the provincial lists of voters, but for some years Sir John Macdonald had chafed under this anomaly. It seemed to him obvious that the parliament of Canada should determine its own electorate, and that the franchise should, as far as possible, be uniform throughout the Dominion. The system in vogue, under which members of the House of Commons were elected under half a dozen different systems, over which parliament had no control, was in his opinion not merely abnormal, but derogatory to the dignity of the superior body. In defence of this system the practice in the United States was sometimes pointed to, but in this matter there was no real analogy between Canada and the United States. The American Union is in reality a federation of sovereign states, of which Congress is the creation. This being the case, it is not incongruous that these states should retain control over congressional elections. But the Canadian provinces are not sovereign; on the contrary, they are, in a real sense, subordinate to the central government.

Sir John Macdonald had also observed, with ever-growing concern, a disposition on the {135} part of some of the provincial legislatures to amend their electoral franchises in a democratic direction. Now, the necessity of a property qualification for the right to vote was ever a first principle with him—the central dogma of his political faith. He said with much energy that no man who favoured manhood suffrage without a property qualification had a right to call himself a Conservative. Once, when Sir John was dwelling on his favourite doctrine in the House of Commons, a member interrupted him to know if he might ask a question. 'Certainly,' replied Sir John. 'Well,' said the member, 'many years ago, during the gold fever, I went out to California, and while there working in the diggings I acquired an interest in a donkey. Under it I voted. Before the next election came round the donkey died, and then I had no vote.... Who voted on the first election, I or the donkey?' It was on the tip of Sir John's tongue to retort that it didn't much matter which, but he forbore, and merely joined in the general laughter.

In conformity with these views Sir John Macdonald introduced his Electoral Franchise Bill in 1883, not with the object of carrying it through parliament that session, but merely {136} for the purpose of placing it before the members. The same thing happened in 1884. But in 1885 the Bill was introduced in earnest. It provided, as far as practicable, for a uniform qualification of voters throughout the Dominion based on property, and also for the registration of voters by revising officers to be appointed by the federal Government. The measure encountered a desperate resistance from the Opposition. For the first time in the parliament of the Dominion there was organized obstruction. On one occasion the House of Commons sat from Thursday afternoon until Saturday midnight, and although this record has since been beaten, it was felt at the time to be a most trying experience. Obstruction was naked and unashamed. Members read long passages from *The Pilgrim's Progress*, or *Robinson Crusoe*, or any other work that happened to appeal to them. One day — the passage is hopelessly buried in Hansard and I cannot find it, but I remember the occasion very vividly — Sir John rose at the opening of the day's proceedings and addressed a few grave and measured words to the Opposition. Starting with the remark that he could only suppose their extraordinary and unparalleled conduct to be the outcome of a misapprehension as to 'my {137} supposed infirmities and my advancing years,' he told them that they were vastly mistaken if they supposed they could tire him out by such methods. He declared that as long as he, and those who acted with him, enjoyed the confidence of the people, they did not intend to resign their functions into the hands of the minority. He begged them, in conclusion, to reflect upon the unwisdom of their course, 'lest what has begun as a farce may end in a tragedy.'

These serious words did not appear to produce any immediate effect, and the debates dragged on through the hot summer months. In the end, however, patience and firmness prevailed, and the Franchise Act reached the statute-book, where it remained until it was repealed twelve years later by the Government of Sir Wilfrid Laurier. The apprehensions of the Opposition with regard to the revising officers were not realized. In Ontario these positions were offered to the county court judges, or to the junior judges, and were accepted by nearly all of them. In the province of Quebec, where there are no county court judges, such appointments were not possible; but the law provided that where the returning officer was not a judge, he must be a barrister or notary of not less than five years' standing, and an appeal in all cases lay from {138} him to a judge. Sir John Macdonald carefully supervised these appointments, which in the great majority of cases were quite unexceptionable. The administration of the Act was no doubt expensive. This was the strongest criticism heard against it; but in the opinion of the Government of that day it was essential to the idea of a united Dominion that the parliament of Canada should determine and control the conditions of acquiring the right to vote for members of its own House of Commons.

88

Sir John A. Macdonald in 1883

I should not omit to state that Sir John professed himself a believer in the extension of the franchise to single women. Apparently he considered that his advocacy of a property qualification required this. I have heard him say, too, that women, as a whole, were conservative, and he considered that their admission to the vote would tend to strengthen the defences against the irruption of an unbridled democracy. Whether these views would have stood the test afforded by the present-day militant suffragettes, I am unable to say; for from Sir John Macdonald the knowledge that there might be something even more disastrous than an unrestrained male democracy was mercifully withheld.

[1] See Pope's *Memoirs of Sir John Macdonald*, vol. i, p. 103.

[2] Dorion voted for the third reading of the Seigneurial Tenure Bill and against that relating to the Clergy Reserves. Brown voted against the third reading of both measures, and the Clear Grits and Rouges as a body did all in their power to impede the passage of both bills.

[3] 'The great reason why I have always been able to beat Brown is that I have been able to look a little ahead, while he could on no occasion forgo the temptation of a temporary triumph' (Sir John A. Macdonald to M. C. Cameron, dated Ottawa, January 3, 1872).

[4] Gladstone stoutly defended the propriety of his course, which had the assent of his whole Cabinet, and also the approval of such great legal authorities as Lords Selborne and Hatherley. This case of Sir Robert Collier is almost exactly on all fours with the 'Double Shuffle.' Gladstone did a similar thing a few months later in the appointment of the Rev. Mr Harvey to the Rectory of Ewelme. See Morley's *Life of Gladstone*, vol. ii, pp. 382-7. For further explanation of the 'Double Shuffle,' see Pope's *Memoirs of Sir John Macdonald*, vol. i, pp. 198-205.

[5] If any one should doubt the ferocity of Brown's attacks on the Ministry, and especially upon Sir John A. Macdonald, let him turn up the *Globe* files for that period—more particularly the issue of

September 5, 1866, which contained an attack so violent as to call forth a protest from so staunch an opponent of the Conservative leader as Alexander Mackenzie. I commend also to the curious the *Globe* of April 30, 1870.

[6] From the Viscount Monck to Mr John A. Macdonald, dated London, May 24, 1867.

[7] Sir John Rose, dated Ottawa, February 23, 1870.

[8] Not the smallest reflection upon Sir Richard Cartwright's personal honour is sought to be conveyed here. Sir John Macdonald himself had been connected with the same institution for many years as shareholder, director, and solicitor, and its failure did not compromise either of them. At the same time, it is obvious that to appoint as Finance minister the president of a bank which had recently closed its doors (no matter for what cause) would be to invite criticism of the most caustic kind.

[9] From Sir John Macdonald to George Stephen, dated Ottawa, December 1, 1869.

[10] From the same to the same, dated Ottawa, December 9, 1869.

[11] From the same to the same, dated Ottawa, December 13, 1869.

[12] *Memoirs of Sir John Macdonald*, vol. ii, pp. 85-140.

[13] From Sir John Macdonald to Sir John Rose, dated Ottawa, March 5, 1872.

[14] To the Viscount Monck, dated Ottawa, October 11, 1872.

[15] For the full text of this letter see Pope's *Memoirs of Sir John Macdonald*, vol. ii, pp. 174-89. In it Macdonald points out:

1. That Canada was under bonds to construct a railway from (say) Montreal to the Pacific.

2. That the House of Commons in the session of 1871, during his absence in Washington, carried a resolution, at the instigation of the Opposition, obliging the Government to build the road through the agency of an incorporated company.

3. That two rival companies—one under Sir Hugh Allan in Montreal, and the other under Mr David Macpherson in Toronto—were formed with the object of securing the charter.

4. That the Government, with a view to removing the great sectional jealousies which had developed between the provinces of Ontario and Quebec, in relation to this matter, endeavoured to secure the amalgamation of these two companies.

5. That while these negotiations were going forward, the general elections of 1872 came on, and, among others, Sir Hugh Allan, as he had done previously for many years, subscribed largely to the Conservative election fund.

6. That Sir Hugh Allan was told before he subscribed a farthing that his railway company would not get the privilege of building the railway. He was informed that the work would only be entrusted to an amalgamated company, under the terms of the Act passed in parliament; that such amalgamation would be effected on terms fair to the provinces of Ontario and Quebec, as agreed upon between the representatives of the two rival companies, and that such amalgamation would take place only after the elections.

7. That under the powers vested in them by the Act, the Government issued a royal charter in which they gave the preponderance of interest to the province of Ontario, according to population. They gave a fair representation to every one of the other provinces, and of the thirteen shareholders and directors of which the company was composed, only one was the nominee or the special choice of Sir Hugh Allan. The others were elected without the slightest reference to him; some of them against his most strenuous opposition, and they included three of the incorporators of the Ontario company, two of whom had been directors in that company. In that charter there were no advantages given, nor could they be given, by the Government. Parliament had decided what the subsidy in money and land should be, and that was given and no more.

[16] At that very time George Brown was writing thus to a leading banker in Toronto:

TORONTO, *August* 15, 1872.

MY DEAR SIR,—The fight goes bravely on.... We have expended our strength in aiding outlying counties and helping our city candidates. But a big push has to be made on Saturday and Monday for the East and West divisions.... We therefore make our grand stand on Saturday. There are but half a dozen people that can come down handsomely, and we have done all we possibly can do, and we have to ask a few outsiders to aid us. Will you be one? I have been urged to write you, and comply accordingly. Things look well all over the Province.... Things look bright in Quebec.—Faithfully yours,

GEO. BROWN.

[17] Senate Debates, 1879, p. 565.

[18] 'I now refer to the diplomatic blunder committed in undertaking solemn engagements that the entire resources of the Empire could not possibly implement.... You will see how unlikely it was that that road, with all the power of man and all the money of Europe, could have been completed in 1881' (Mackenzie at Sarnia, October 11, 1875).

Even after the completion of the C.P.R. the *Globe* mocked at the enterprise in this fashion: 'The iron band of Confederation has been completed.... The salubrious Rocky and Selkirk ranges may now become a summer resort for the fashionable and crowded populations situated between Callander and Rat Portage. In short, the Canadian Pacific Railway has been opened.... For our own part, we have not the slightest doubt that the C.P.R. will be no less effective than the N.P. in creating wealth for Canada.... This will be amply proved by the spectacle of a railway 2500 miles long operated on the strength of a traffic with about 150,000 people. Such a thing was never tried before, and is unlikely ever to be tried again' (*Globe*, July 13, 1886).

[19] 'You don't, I think, give sufficient weight to the troubles and difficulties which beset the Government, and you have exaggerated our power—forgetting that we have a strong opposition and a watchful press which charge us with being mere tools of the C.P.R., and not knowing that more than once we were deserted by our own parliamentary friends in caucus, and that it was only my individual power over them that enabled us on more than one occasion to

come to your relief (Sir John Macdonald to Sir George Stephen, dated August 1, 1890).

[20] This was the Hon. P. Landry, the present speaker (1915) of the Senate. He was a fast friend and supporter of Macdonald, but he disapproved of the execution of Riel.

{139}

CHAPTER III

OLD AGE

'With the Canadian Pacific Railway finished, and my Franchise Bill become law, I feel that I have done my work and can now sing my *Nunc dimittis*.'

So wrote Sir John Macdonald to Lord Carnarvon shortly after the close of the arduous parliamentary session of 1885. There can be little doubt that these words expressed his inmost sentiments at the time. He had passed the allotted span of threescore years and ten, had 'sounded all the depths and shoals of honour,' and was beginning to look forward to a brief period of freedom from the cares of state before he should be too old to enjoy it. His great work was done. The scattered colonies had been united into a vast Dominion. The great North-West and the Pacific province had been added and Canada now extended from ocean to ocean, its several provinces joined together by iron {140} bands. The reader of these pages can form some idea of the difficulties, of the labours, the anxieties, and the discouragements encountered in the execution of this giant task; and also of the marvellous courage, patience, and endurance which sustained the master builder throughout, and eventually enabled him to triumph over all opposition. Small wonder that Sir John Macdonald, with the consciousness of duty faithfully performed, sometimes in later life yearned for that rest which he was fated never to enjoy.

Party considerations forbade it. Macdonald's political friends could not reconcile themselves to his retirement, and he, in turn, could not make up his mind to abandon them. They declared that his withdrawal meant the certain disintegration and consequent defeat of the great party which he had built up, the party whose destinies he had so long guided. There were, moreover, at this particular time special reasons which rendered his controlling hand more than ever necessary. It was no secret that the French-Canadian ministers, Langevin, Caron, and Chapleau, were far from showing that spirit of mutual trust and confidence which is supposed to exist among members of the same Ministry. {141} Sir Hector Langevin, the senior of the triumvirate, had been the lieutenant of Cartier, but, in this instance, the mantle of Elijah had not fallen upon his successor. In my experience I never met a man who more neatly fulfilled Bismarck's cynical description of Lord Salisbury — 'a lath painted to look like iron.' He was a good departmental officer — but he was nothing more. The moment Sir John Macdonald's support was taken away, he fell. Yet Sir John stood by him against the attacks of his opponents, and generally sided with him in his differences with his colleagues.

During a holiday of 1888 Sir John said to me one day at Dalhousie, N.B., where he was spending the summer: 'George Stephen keeps pressing me to retire, and I think I shall. My only difficulty is about my successor.' 'Whom do you think of as such?' I asked. 'Oh,' replied he, 'Langevin; there is no one else.'[1] 'Well,' I remarked, 'I have a candidate — one who lives on the border line between the two provinces, speaks both languages with facility, and is equally at home {142} in Quebec and Ontario.' 'Who is he?' 'Mr Abbott,' I replied. 'John Abbott,' said Sir John incredulously. 'Why, he hasn't a single qualification for the office. Thompson,' he went on, 'is very able and a fine fellow, but Ontario would never endure his turning Catholic. No, I see no one but Langevin.' Yet it was Abbott after all. When asked why he thought so much of Langevin, the reply was at once forthcoming: 'He has always been true to me.' The same thing might have been said of Sir Adolphe Caron, ever a faithful supporter, and from his youth up, equally in prosperity and adversity, a close personal friend of the old chief; but Sir John thought that Caron sometimes allowed his personal feelings to obscure his judgment, or, as he expressed it, 'Caron is too much influenced by his hates — a fatal mistake in a public man, who should have no resentments.' Sir Adolphe Chapleau, with all his attractiveness and charm, Sir John never quite trusted. The relations between these three French-Canadian ministers were hard to define. I frankly confess that, with all my opportunities, I could never master the intricacies of Lower-Canadian politics in those days. In the beginning it seemed to be a case of Langevin and {143} Caron against Chapleau; later it sometimes looked as though Langevin and Chapleau were making common cause against Caron; perhaps most often it resembled a triangular duel. There was absolutely no difference between those three men in respect of public policy, but the personal jealousy and suspicion with which they regarded one another was amusing.

'Langevin,' said Sir John, 'on his way down to Quebec, cannot stop off for lunch at Montreal, but Chapleau writes me that he is interfering in his district, and if he leaves his house in Quebec for a walk down John Street, Caron wires in cypher that a breach in the party is imminent.' Langevin, on his part, was equally vigilant to resent the encroachments, real or supposed, of his colleagues upon his domain, and altogether Sir John had no pleasant time keeping the peace among them.

In the English section of the Cabinet three vacancies had recently taken place. Immediately after the close of the session of 1885 considerations of health compelled Sir David Macpherson to give up the portfolio of the Interior. This in no sense interfered with the personal and political friendship which had long existed between him and his leader. Sir David, albeit over cautious and deliberate in {144} his methods, was a man of good judgment, and wholly animated by a desire for the public good. His administrative record suffered from his delays in settling the grievances of the half-breeds of the North-West. This had afforded Riel the pretext for the second rising, but how far responsibility in this matter properly attached to Macpherson, I am not prepared to say.

Sir David Macpherson was succeeded in the office of minister of the Interior by Thomas White, a well-known Conservative journalist of Montreal, where he and his brother Richard conducted the Montreal *Gazette*. For many years White had been a faithful exponent of Conservative principles in the press. In his efforts to enter parliament he had been singularly unfortunate. In 1867 he had been defeated in South Wentworth by three votes; in 1874 in Prescott by six votes; in 1875 in Montreal West by seven votes; and in the following year in the same constituency by fifty votes. Finally, he was elected in 1878 for the then existing electoral division of Cardwell, in the province of Ontario. Seven years later he became a colleague of the chieftain whose cause he had so long and so effectively promoted. To the great grief of {145} Sir John Macdonald, White died within three years of taking office. Few statesmen of so great merit have experienced such persistent ill fortune. Had he lived, he might not improbably have become prime minister of Canada.

In the autumn of 1885 the minister of Finance, Sir Leonard Tilley, resigned to become lieutenant-governor of New Brunswick. In another volume I have alluded to his close friendship with Sir John Macdonald. If White was an unlucky politician, assuredly the same cannot be said of Sir Leonard Tilley. In 1867 he gave up the office of prime minister of New Brunswick to enter the Dominion Cabinet; he remained minister until a few days before the downfall of 1873, when he was appointed lieutenant-governor of New Brunswick. This post he held throughout the period when the Conservatives were in opposition (1873 to 1878). Upon the return of the party to power in 1878, Tilley, having just completed his term as lieutenant-governor, became minister of Finance. After holding this office for seven years, he slipped back again into the post of lieutenant-governor of New Brunswick. Sir Leonard's place in the Cabinet was taken by Mr (now Sir) George {146} E. Foster, whose signal ability was thus recognized thirty years ago by Sir John Macdonald.

In May 1884 Sir Charles Tupper relinquished the portfolio of Railways and Canals in order to devote himself exclusively to the office of high commissioner for Canada in London, to which he had been appointed a year before. It is unnecessary to say that the withdrawal of Sir Charles from the Cabinet, in which he had so long exercised a commanding influence, proved a serious loss. Indeed, as the sequel shows, his presence became so necessary that he had to return. Sir John Macdonald's choice of a successor from Nova Scotia fell upon Mr Justice (afterwards Sir John) Thompson, a brilliant man, who will never be appreciated at his true worth because his term of office was too short. The selection was at variance with Sir John's expressed views on the inexpediency of judges leaving the bench to return to political life, but it proved singularly happy, and in time Thompson became prime minister. 'Thompson,' observed Macdonald, 'has just two faults. He is a little too fond of satire, and a little too much of a Nova Scotian.' It cannot be denied that, in spite of Thompson's great ability, his point of view remained {147} provincial to the end. In his heart of hearts Nova Scotia rather than Canada ever held first place. No more upright man ever breathed. He had a fierce intolerance of the slightest departure from absolute rectitude. The case of a chief clerk in the Civil Service, who had committed serious irregularities in connection with the public funds, once came up before the Cabinet. Thompson, always severe in such matters, considered that the gravity of the offence called for dismissal, but to this Macdonald would not consent, holding that reduction in rank to a first-class clerkship, with corresponding loss of salary, would be sufficient punishment. It was seldom that Macdonald, in the ordinary course of administration, interposed his paramount authority as first minister, but, though the Council as a whole rather inclined towards Thompson's view, Macdonald insisted that the more merciful punishment should be imposed. Thompson was angry, but said nothing more at the time. Not long afterwards a third-class railway mail clerk, with a salary of $500 a year, got into similar trouble. 'What shall be done with this man?' asked Macdonald at the Council Board. There was a moment's pause, which was broken by the bland {148} suggestion from Thompson that, 'following precedent, he be made a first-class clerk.'

Thompson had a caustic wit. A certain inventor of Toronto, who had devised an ingenious means for safeguarding level railway crossings, had long bombarded Sir John Macdonald with applications for Government patronage. When Sir John became minister of Railways in 1889, the inventor thought that his day had at last arrived. He went post-haste to Ottawa, obtained the requisite permission, and installed his models in a room belonging to the Railway department. One day Macdonald and Thompson happened to come along the corridor going to Macdonald's office. The inventor, who had been lying in wait, pressed them to step aside for a minute and inspect his models. Sir John, seeing no escape, said to his companion, 'Come along, Thompson, and let us see what this fellow's got to show us.' Thompson hated mechanical contrivances, but there was no way out of it, so he followed the chief. The delighted inventor felt that he had at last realized his desire, and was in great form. He volubly descanted on the frequent loss of life at level crossings and proceeded to show his devices for lessening such dangers. The day was {149} piping hot and he had taken off his coat. He rushed round the table and touched bells here and there, which caused gates to close and open, semaphores to drop, and all sorts of things to happen. As the ministers took their leave, Macdonald said to his companion, 'Well, Thompson, what do you think of that chap?' 'I think,' replied Thompson with great energy, 'that he deserves to be killed on a level crossing.'

Once, while Lord Aberdeen was governor-general, Sir John Thompson was dining at Government House on an evening in June when the mosquitoes were unusually troublesome. Lady Aberdeen suggested the shutting of the windows. 'Oh! thank you,' replied Sir John, 'pray don't trouble; I think they are all in now!'

Sir Alexander Campbell was from youth intimately connected with Sir John Macdonald — as a fellow-citizen of Kingston, as law student and subsequently as partner in a legal firm, as a colleague for many years in the government of the old province of Canada and afterwards in that of the Dominion. Yet the two were never kindred spirits. Sir Alexander Campbell was a Tory aristocrat, a veritable grand seigneur, of dignified bearing {150} and courtly mien. He made an excellent minister of Justice, but he lacked that *bonhomie* which so endeared Sir John Macdonald to the multitude. I do not think that Sir John's pre-eminence in that direction ever gave Sir Alexander much concern. My impression is that he regarded the multitude as an assemblage of more or less uninteresting persons, necessary only at election times; and if Sir John could succeed in obtaining their votes, he was quite welcome to any incidental advantages that he might extract from the process. It was alleged by Sir Richard Cartwright that in the year 1864 a movement was started in the Conservative party with the object of supplanting Macdonald and putting Campbell in his place, and that Sir John never forgave Campbell for his part in this affair. Something of the kind was talked about at the date mentioned, but the movement proved a complete fiasco, and it is not at all clear that Campbell was a consenting party to it. I doubt too the correctness of Sir Richard's inference, for, leaving the 1864 incident out of account, there never was the slightest political division between the two men. At the time of the Pacific Scandal, Campbell behaved exceedingly {151} well to his chief. Yet, speaking of the period within my own knowledge — that is to say, during the last ten years of Macdonald's life — while ever externally friends, the two in their personal relations were antipathetic. This may in part be ascribed to Campbell's dignified love of ease and disinclination to join in the rough-and-tumble of party politics. When elections were to be fought (I speak only of my own time) Campbell, if he did not find that he had business elsewhere, was disposed to look on in a patronizing sort of way. He seldom took off his coat or even his gloves in the fight, but he always turned up when the victory was won. Sir John resented this. Yet assuredly Campbell had some merits, or Macdonald would not have kept him in successive Cabinets. Sir Alexander was an ideal leader of the Senate, and this qualification alone rendered him of much value. He was, moreover, *par excellence* the aristocrat of the Cabinet, and such a type of public man is rare in Canada.

The antithesis of Sir Alexander Campbell was John Henry Pope, sometime minister of Agriculture and later of Railways and Canals. Pope was a man of small education and less culture, but of great natural ability, and was {152} gifted with remarkable political sagacity. Macdonald used to say that Pope could have been anything he desired had he only received a good education in his youth. He added that he had never known Pope's judgment to be at fault. In times of stress and difficulty Pope was the colleague of whom he first sought advice and counsel, and upon whose rough good sense he implicitly relied. Pope died two years before his chief, who never ceased to mourn his loss.

Another self-made colleague of the same stamp was Mr Frank Smith of Toronto. Mr Smith was a member of the Cabinet from 1882 to 1891, during which long period his keen business sagacity and sound common sense were ever at his chief's disposal.

Sir Mackenzie Bowell, 'the best Minister of Customs I ever had,' was another old-time friend and colleague for whom Sir John entertained a high regard and respect. Sir Mackenzie's chief claims to prominence are of a date subsequent to the day of Sir John Macdonald and therefore do not fall within the compass of this work; but he is one who in serene old age remains a connecting link with those stirring times.

The pre-eminence of Sir Charles Tupper {153} must not lead me to forget that his son had the honour of being one of Sir John's colleagues in the old chieftain's latter years. Sir Charles Hibbert Tupper became a Cabinet minister at thirty-two, the same age as that at which the youthful John A. Macdonald had entered the Cabinet of

Draper, forty-one years before. During the years in which the younger Tupper held the office of minister of Marine and Fisheries he made an enviable record as an efficient and courageous administrator. I fancy Sir John used sometimes to think that he was perhaps more particular about the administration of patronage in his own department than in those of his colleagues. One day, shortly after Mr Tupper (as he was then) had become a minister, he sent a letter from some applicant for office over to Sir John with the request that if possible he would do something for the writer. Sir John took the letter, folded it, endorsed it, 'Dear Charlie, skin your own skunks. Yours always, J. A. M.D.,' and sent it back to the new minister; as much as to say, 'Now that you have a department of your own, look after these people yourself.'

Mr John Costigan was a member of Sir John Macdonald's Cabinet from 1882 till 1891. {154} Shortly after the appearance of my *Memoirs of Sir John Macdonald*, Mr Costigan publicly stated that I had made a mistake in saying that Macdonald had not been in favour of Home Rule for Ireland. Goldwin Smith declared, indeed, that Sir John Macdonald had no settled convictions upon Home Rule, but was ever ready to propitiate the Irish vote by any sacrifice of principle that might be required. That Sir John reduced the original Home Rule resolutions before the Dominion parliament in 1882 and 1886 to mere expressions of contingent hope, such (to use Goldwin Smith's own words) 'as any Unionist might have subscribed,'[2] and that Macdonald voted against Mr Curran's substantive resolution in favour of Home Rule in 1887, when he could not modify it, was as well known to Goldwin Smith as to Mr Costigan. In addition, Goldwin Smith possessed indubitable evidence, at first hand, of Sir John Macdonald's sentiments on the subject of Home Rule. During the political campaign of 1886-87 Goldwin Smith said some hard things of Sir John and the Conservative party. He was at the same time attacking Gladstone very bitterly on his Home Rule policy. Some {155} weeks after the Canadian elections were over, Sir John Macdonald visited Toronto, and stayed at the Queen's Hotel. Among the visitors on the day of his arrival was Goldwin Smith, who, as he entered the room, murmured something about the doubtful propriety of making a social call upon one whom he felt it his duty to oppose in the recent contest. Sir John Macdonald held out both hands saying, 'My dear sir, I forgive you everything for your splendid defence of the Empire,' alluding to his attacks on Home Rule. This remark and the conversation which ensued made quite clear where Sir John Macdonald stood on the question of Home Rule—a position which he never compromised by any word or act. To assert the contrary implies a charge of opportunism; but Goldwin Smith himself, when calmly analysing Macdonald's character sixteen years after his death, deliberately asserted that 'if he [Sir John] was partisan, he was not opportunist.'[3] Goldwin Smith knew right well that Sir John Macdonald was just as resolutely opposed as he was himself to the establishment of a separate parliament in Dublin with an executive responsible thereto. On the evening of the day just mentioned {156} Macdonald dined with Goldwin Smith. As we drove to 'The Grange' Sir John asked me if I had ever been there before. I had not.

'Well,' said he, 'you are going to a very interesting house with a charming host, but notice Mr Smith's habit of interlarding his otherwise agreeable conversation with tiresome references to the nobility. Why, to hear him talk, you would imagine he never consorted in England with anybody under the rank of an earl.' Later that evening, as we went to the station to take our train, Sir John said, 'Did you observe what I told you? That's why Dizzy in *Lothair* called him a social parasite. Strange that so brilliant a man, who needs no adventitious aids, should manifest such a weakness.'

In the autumn of 1886 Sir John Macdonald, accompanied by four of his colleagues—Chapleau, White, Thompson, and Foster—made a tour of the province of Ontario, towards the close of which he wrote thus to Sir Charles Tupper:

I am on my way back to Ottawa after a successful tour in Western Ontario. We have made a very good impression, and I think will hold our own in the Province. {157} We have, however, lost nearly the whole of the Catholic vote by the course of the *Mail*, and this course has had a prejudicial effect not only in Ontario but throughout the Dominion, and has therefore introduced a great element of uncertainty in a good many constituencies.

In Nova Scotia the outlook is bad, and the only hope of our holding our own there is your immediate return and vigorous action. It may be necessary that you should, even if only for a time, return to the Cabinet. M'Lelan, I know, would readily make way for you. Now, the responsibility on you is very great, for should any disaster arise because of your not coming out, the whole blame will be thrown upon you.

I see that Anglin is now starring it in Nova Scotia. I send you an extract from a condensed report of his remarks which appeared in the Montreal *Gazette*. This is a taking programme for the Maritime Provinces and has to be met, and no one can do it but yourself. But enough of Dominion politics.

I cannot in conclusion too strongly press upon you the absolute necessity of your {158} coming out at once, and do not like to contemplate the evil consequences of your declining to do so.

I shall cable you the time for holding our election the moment it is settled.

That the general elections of 1887 were fought with exceeding bitterness may be inferred from a paragraph in a leading Canadian newspaper of the day:

Now W. M. Tweed [the criminal 'boss' in New York] was an abler scoundrel than is Sir John Macdonald. He was more courageous, if possible more unscrupulous, and more crafty, and he had himself, as he thought, impregnably entrenched. Yet in a few short months he was in a prison cell deserted and despised by all who had lived upon his wickedness — and there he died.

This of course is a mere exhibition of partisan rage and spite. It contains no single word or phrase in the smallest degree applicable to Sir John Macdonald, who, far from being dishonest, was ever scrupulously fair and just in all his dealings, both public and private. This, I am persuaded, is now well {159} understood. What is not so well known is that he disliked extravagance of any kind. He was, it is true, a man of bold conceptions, and when convinced that a large policy was in the interest of the country, he never hesitated at its cost. Thus he purchased the North-West, built the Canadian Pacific Railway, and spent millions on canals. But in the ordinary course of affairs he was prudent, even economical, and as careful of public money as of his own. At the close of a long life he spoke of the very modest competence he had provided for his family as having been 'painfully and laboriously saved.'

If Sir John's critic, quoted above, meant to convey the idea that in 1887 Sir John thought himself firmly entrenched in power, he was far from the mark. For Sir John went into the elections of 1887 believing that he would be defeated. The Riel movement in the province of Quebec had assumed formidable proportions, and the fatuous course of former Conservative allies, Dalton M'Carthy and the *Mail* newspaper, in raising an anti-French and anti-Catholic cry threatened disaster in Ontario. The friendly provincial Government in Quebec had been overthrown in October 1886, and in the following {160} December Oliver Mowat, in the hope of strengthening the hands of Blake, then leading the Ottawa Opposition, suddenly dissolved the Ontario legislature. Mowat was successful in his own appeal. But, strange to say, the local triumph probably injured rather than aided Blake. At least such was Sir John's opinion. He held that his attitude on the Home Rule question had alienated a goodly proportion of the Irish vote which usually went with him, and that these people, having taken the edge off their resentment by voting Liberal in the provincial elections, felt free to return to their political allegiance when the Dominion elections came on two months later. This sounds far-fetched, but it was the opinion of a man who had been studying political elections in Ontario all his long life. At any rate, Sir John Macdonald carried fifty-four out of ninety-two seats in Ontario; and Edward Blake was so discouraged by the result that on the meeting of the new parliament he resigned the leadership of the Opposition in favour of Mr Laurier.

Of Sir Wilfrid Laurier and his subsequent career it does not devolve upon me to speak. I will only say that if his predecessors in the {161} leadership of the Liberal party, for one cause or another, failed to realize the hopes of their political followers, he amply made up for their shortcomings by achieving signal success. Fortune, no doubt, was kinder to him than to them, but, apart from all other questions, Sir Wilfrid's personal qualities had no small influence in bringing about his party triumphs. Alike in Opposition and in power, his unfailing tact, old-fashioned courtesy, conciliatory methods, urbanity, moderation, and unvarying good temper evoked the sympathy of thousands whom Blake's coldly intellectual feats failed to attract and Mackenzie's rigidity of demeanour served only to repel. Simultaneously with Mr Laurier's advent to the leadership of the Opposition in 1887, a moderating influence began to be felt in the House of Commons, which gradually affected the whole tone of political life in Canada, until the old-time bitterness of party strife in a large measure passed away.

About a month before Sir John Macdonald died Mr Laurier came to his office in the House of Commons to discuss some question of adjournment. When he had gone, the chief said to me, 'Nice chap that. If I were twenty years younger, he'd be my colleague.' {162} 'Perhaps he may be yet, sir,' I remarked. Sir John shook his head. 'Too old,' said he, 'too old,' and passed into the inner room.

I must not omit an amusing incident which happened in the autumn of 1888. During the summer of that year Honoré Mercier, the Liberal prime minister of Quebec, had called upon Sir John at the Inch Arran hotel at Dalhousie, New Brunswick. It was the first time they had met, and Mercier, who showed a disposition to be friendly, asked Sir John if he would give him an interview with himself and his colleagues at Ottawa in order to discuss some financial questions outstanding between the Dominion and the province. Sir John promised to do so, and when he returned to town fixed a day for the meeting. In the preceding July the Quebec legislature had passed the once famous Jesuits' Estates Act. This Act was then before Sir John's Cabinet and he was under strong pressure to disallow it. While Sir John had no love for Mercier or his Government, and while he thought the preamble of the Jesuits' Estates Act, with its ostentatious references to the Pope, highly objectionable, he had no doubt that the Act was wholly within the competence of the {163} Quebec legislature and was not a subject for disallowance. Obviously Quebec could do what it liked with its own money. Sir John was having much trouble at the time with several of the provincial legislatures, which were showing a disposition to encroach upon the federal domain. It was necessary that he should walk warily, lest he should put himself in the wrong by interfering with legislation clearly within the power of provincial legislatures. He was persuaded that the obnoxious phrases in the preamble of the Jesuits' Estates Act had been inserted with the express object of tempting him to an arbitrary and unjust exercise of power which would react disastrously upon him, not only in Quebec, but also in Ontario, Manitoba, and elsewhere. It was all too palpable, and, as he used to say, 'in vain is the net spread in the sight of any bird.'

Mercier's visit, however, had no relation to this matter, but had been arranged for the discussion of purely financial matters with Sir John and his colleagues. The appointed morning arrived, and Mercier, frock-coated and very formal and precise, was shown into Sir John's office. A meeting of Council had been called for the occasion, and while the members {164} were gathering the two leaders exchanged a few remarks of a purely conventional character. At length, when all was ready, Sir John rose and, with a stiff bow and 'Will you follow me, sir?' led the way along the hall towards the council chamber, with Mercier close behind him. As they turned into the corridor leading to the chamber, Mercier, feeling some constraint and wishing to make a little conversation, said, half jokingly, 'Sir John, I wish you would tell us whether you are going to disallow our Jesuits' Estates Act or not.' Suddenly the old man unbent, his eyes brightened, his features grew mobile, as he half looked back over his shoulder and said in a stage whisper, 'Do you take me for a damn fool?' In a second it was all over, his figure again became erect, all trace of expression died out of his face, and with measured pace and serious mien the two men passed into the council chamber.

My recollections of the day of Sir John Macdonald are chiefly connected with official, as distinct from parliamentary, life. At the same time I recall many amusing incidents which took place in the House of Commons. Of all the members of that assembly I thought Sir Richard Cartwright the most accomplished {165} debater. He was perhaps the only member of the House who could afford to have his words taken down and printed exactly as he spoke them. Uniformly a kind and considerate minister towards his subordinates, his attitude towards his opponents in parliament was ferocious, though perhaps this ferocity was often more simulated than real. One illustration of his savage humour occurs to me. About the year 1883 a life of Sir John Macdonald appeared written by a certain John Edmund Collins. Sir John did not know the author, nor had he any connection with the book. It was merely a well-ordered presentation of facts already known, and did not profess to be anything more. Some of the government departments bought copies and the title appeared in the public accounts, which came before parliament. This gave Sir Richard one of those opportunities to attack Sir John of which he never failed to take advantage. After saying some disagreeable things, he concluded thus: 'However, Mr Speaker, I am bound to say that I think it quite fit that a gentleman who in his day has done justice to so many John Collinses, should at last have a John Collins to do justice to him.' To the uninitiated it may be explained {166} that 'John Collins' is the name of a rather potent beverage.

This pointed allusion to Sir John's convivial habits leads me to say, in all candour, that his failings in this regard were greatly exaggerated. There is no doubt that at one time—in an age when almost everybody drank wine freely—he was no exception to the general rule. This was particularly true of the period of his widowerhood, between 1857 and 1867, when his lapses were such as occasionally to interfere with his public duties. But certainly during the last ten years of his life (and probably for a longer period) his habits were most temperate. His principal beverages were milk and at dinner a glass of claret. I rarely knew him to touch spirits, and if he did so now and then, it was in great moderation.

Sir John Macdonald never seems to have felt towards Sir Richard Cartwright the degree of bitterness that marked Cartwright's pursuit of him. I do not pretend to say that he liked him, but he was always fair. This letter to an over-zealous supporter may perhaps serve as an illustration.

OTTAWA, 28*th March* 1891.

DEAR SIR,—I have yours of the 23rd instant informing me that Sir Richard {167} Cartwright is going to Kingston to inquire into some matters with regard to the Provincial penitentiary. He has a right to do so as a member of Parliament, nor do I think that any impediment should be thrown in his way. If there be any irregularities committed in the penitentiary, there are no reasons why they should be hidden, and the parties committing irregularities properly dealt with. — I am, dear sir, yours very truly,

JOHN A. MACDONALD.

No sketch of the House of Commons of those days, however brief, should omit mention of Alonzo Wright, the 'King of the Gatineau,' as he was commonly known. Wright was a genial, whole-souled plutocrat of the old school. He represented the county of Ottawa, and resided on the banks of the Gatineau river, where his hospitable doors were ever open to his many friends. He was an old-fashioned Tory, but never took politics very seriously. Sometimes, indeed, he showed symptoms of independence, but, as Sir John used laughingly to say, 'while Alonzo's speeches are sometimes wrong, his vote is always right.' Sir John, of course, was quite {168} satisfied with this arrangement. Once a year, to the great entertainment of the House, Wright would make a characteristic speech, felicitously phrased and brimful of humour. One of these harangues in particular remains in my recollection. Like all good-natured members residing near the capital, 'Alonzo' was much plagued by office-seekers of all classes. Among these was a certain Madame Laplante of Hull, whose aspirations did not rise above a charwoman's place. She was unusually persistent. One day, as the 'King' was driving over the Sappers Bridge, he saw a woman in front of his horses waving her arms wildly as a signal to stop. He pulled up, and saw that it was Madame Laplante. Being rather hazy as to her present fortunes, he ventured to express the hope that she liked the position which he had been so fortunate as to obtain for her. Madame Laplante, with sobs, said that she was still without work. At this the 'King' feigned unbounded indignation. The rest must be told in his own words.

'Impossible,' I made answer. 'It cannot be.' Upon receiving renewed assurances that so it was, my resolution was {169} taken in an instant. Turning my carriage I bade the weeping woman enter, and drove at once to the Public Departments. Brushing aside the minions who sought to arrest our progress, I strode unannounced into the Ministerial presence. 'Sir,' said I, 'I have come to you as a suitor for the last time. You may remember that you promised me that this worthy woman should be employed forthwith. I learn to-day that that promise, like many others you have made me, is still unfulfilled. There is a time when patience ceases to be a virtue. Sir, my resolution is taken. I am as good a party man as lives, but there is something that I value more than my party, and that is my self-respect. This afternoon my resignation shall be in the hands of the Speaker, and I shall then be free to state publicly the sentiments I entertain towards all violators of their word, and by the aid of this victim of duplicity, to expose your perfidious treatment of one of your hitherto most faithful supporters.' My arguments, my entreaties, my threats prevailed, and Madame Laplante that day entered the service of her country, which she continues to adorn!

{170}

Many delightful stories are told of Macdonald's ally, Lord Strathcona. I have room for only two. A seedy-looking person named M'Donald once called at the high commissioner's office in London. When asked the nature of his business, he replied that he was in straitened circumstances, and that when Lord Strathcona, as young Donald Smith, had left Forres in Scotland for America, he had been driven to the port whence he sailed by his present visitor's father. When the secretary had duly informed Lord Strathcona of this, word was given to admit M'Donald. Presently the bell rang, and the secretary appeared. 'Make out a cheque for £5 in favour of Mr M'Donald,' said Lord Strathcona. This was done, and M'Donald went on his way rejoicing. In a month or so he turned up again; the same thing happened, and again he departed with a five-pound cheque. This went on for several months; but M'Donald came once too often. On the occasion of his last visit Lord Strathcona did not happen to be in a complaisant mood. When M'Donald was announced he said to the secretary: 'Tell him I'll not see him. And as for Mr M'Donald's father having driven me from Forres when I went to America, {171} it is not true, sir! *I walked, sir!*' — the last three words with tremendous emphasis.

During one of Donald Smith's election contests in Manitoba he felt some uneasiness as to the probable course of a knot of half-breeds in his constituency, but was assured by his election agent that these people were being 'looked after,' and that he need not have any apprehension in regard to them. This agent belonged to a class of westerners noted for the vigour rather than for the correctness of their language. Smith himself, as is well known, was always most proper in this respect. Now, it so happened that in the last hours of the campaign the half-breeds who were the objects of his solicitude were beguiled by the enemy, and that they voted against Smith, who lost the election. He felt this defeat very keenly, and so did his agent, who had to bear the additional mortification of having unintentionally misled his principal. When the results of the polling were announced, the agent relieved his feelings by denouncing the delinquent half-breeds in true Hudson's Bay style, and at every opprobrious and profane epithet Smith was heard to murmur with sympathetic approval, 'Are they not, Mr − −? are they not? are they not?'

{172}

During the period between 1887 and 1891 the Opposition developed the policy of unrestricted reciprocity with the United States, which they made the chief feature of their policy in the general elections of the latter year. Sir John Macdonald opposed this policy with all the energy at his command. He held that it would inevitably lead to the absorption of Canada by the United States, though he did not believe that this was the desire or the intention of its chief promoters. Sir John feared too that the cry would prove seductive. In the hope of arresting the movement before it had more fully advanced, he dissolved parliament prematurely and appealed to the people in mid-winter. In this resolve he was perhaps influenced by a growing consciousness of his failing physical strength. He was less pessimistic as to the result of the election than in 1887, yet he considered his chances of success not more than even. As on previous occasions, he had recourse to Sir Charles Tupper, to whom he cabled on January 21, 1891: 'Your presence during election contest in Maritime Provinces essential to encourage our friends. Please come. Answer.'

The old war-horse, who doubtless had {173} scented the battle from afar, was not slow in responding to his leader's appeal. The contest was severe, and on Sir John's part was fought almost single-handed. His Ontario colleagues were too busy in defending their own seats to render him much assistance in the province at large. It was on this occasion that he issued his famous manifesto to the people of Canada containing the well-known phrase: 'A British subject I was born, a British subject I will die.' In this manifesto he earnestly exhorted the electors to reject a policy which, he was per-suaded, would imperil their British allegiance. The people who had so often sustained him in the past responded to his fervent appeal, and again he was victorious. Nor had he to wait long for a signal confirmation of his estimate of the policy of his opponents. On the day after the polling Edward Blake published a letter to his constit-uents in West Durham, unsparingly condemning unrestricted reci-procity as tending towards annexation to the United States — 'a pre-cursor of political Union' — of which he was unable to approve, and in consequence of which he retired from public life.

Macdonald had won, but it was his last triumph. The wheel had gone full circle, {174} and he, who in the flush of youth had begun his political career with the announcement of his firm resolve to resist, from whatever quarter it might come, any attempt which might tend to weaken the union between Canada and the mother country, fittingly closed it forty-seven years later by an appeal to the people of the Dominion to aid him in his last effort 'for the unity of the Empire and the preservation of our commercial and political freedom.' He won, but the effort proved too great for his waning vitality, and within three months of his victory he passed away.

In *The Times* of September 1, 1903, Dr L. S. (now Sir Starr) Jame-son published this letter from Cecil Rhodes to Sir John Macdonald:

CAPE TOWN, *8th May* 1891.

DEAR SIR, — I wished to write and congratulate you on winning the elections in Canada. I read your manifesto and I could under-stand the issue. If I might express a wish, it would be that we could meet before our stern fate claims us. I might write pages, but I feel I know you and your politics as if we had been friends for years. The whole thing lies in the {175} question, Can we invent some tie with our mother country that will prevent separation? It must be a practical one, for future generations will not be born in England. The curse is that English politicians cannot see the future. They think they will always be the manufacturing mart of the world, but do not understand what protection coupled with reciprocal relations means. I have taken the liberty of writing to you; if you honour me with an answer I will write again. —

Yours,
C. J. RHODES.

PS. You might not know who I am, so I will say I am the Prime Minister of this Colony — that is the Cape Colony.

Sir John Macdonald never received this letter. It was written in South Africa in May, and Sir John died on June 6.

Sir John Macdonald's resemblance to Lord Beaconsfield has often been remarked. That it must have been striking is evident from Sir Charles Dilke's comment:

The first time I saw Sir John Macdonald was shortly after Lord Beaconsfield's death and as the clock struck midnight. I was {176} starting from Euston station, and there appeared at the step of the railway carriage, in Privy Councillor's uniform (the right to wear which is confined to so small a number of persons that one expects to know by sight those who wear it), a figure precisely similar to that of the late Conservative leader, and it required, indeed, a severe exercise of presence of mind to remember that there had been a City banquet from which the apparition must be coming, and rapidly to arrive by a process of exhaustion at the knowledge that this twin brother of that Lord Beaconsfield whom shortly before I had seen in the sick room, which he was not to leave, must be the Prime Minister of Canada.[4]

At an evening reception in London, Sir John, who was standing a little apart, saw a lady attract another's attention, saying in an earnest whisper, 'You say you have never seen Lord Beaconsfield. There he is,' pointing to Sir John.

Sir John Macdonald's underlying and controlling thought was ever for the British Empire. That Canada should exist separate {177} and apart from England was a contingency he never contemplated. The bare mention of such a possibility always evoked his strongest condemnation as being fatal to the realization of a united Empire, which was the dominant aspiration of his life.[5] To see Canada, Australia, and South Africa united by ties of loyalty, affection, and material interest; to see them ranged round the mother country as a protection and a defence — to see the dear land of England secure, to see her strong in every quarter of the globe, mistress of the seas, 'with the waves rolling about her feet, {178} happy in her children and her children blessed in her' — such was Sir John Macdonald's dearest wish. As his devoted wife has most truly written of him:

Through all the fever, the struggles, the battles, hopes and fears, disappointments and successes, joys and sorrows, anxieties and rewards of those long busy years, this fixed idea of an united Empire was his guiding star and inspiration. I, who can speak with something like authority on this point, declare that I do not think any man's mind could be more fully possessed {179} of an overwhelming strong principle than was this man's mind of this principle. It was the 'Empire' and 'England's precedent' always, in things great and small — from the pattern of a ceremony, or the spelling of a word, to the shaping of laws and the modelling of a constitution. With a courage at once fierce and gentle, generally in the face of tremendous opposition, often against dangerous odds, he carried measure after measure in the Canadian Parliament, each measure a stone in the edifice of empire which he so passionately believed in and was so proud to help build and rear.[6]

A parliamentary federation of the Empire he considered impracticable. He did not believe that the people of Canada — or of any other dependency of Great Britain — would ever consent to be taxed by a central body sitting outside its borders, nor did he relish the idea that the mother of parliaments at Westminster should be subordinated to any federal legislature, no matter how dignified and important it might be. He believed in allowing Canada's relations with the mother {180} country to remain as they are. To use his own words, spoken within a year or so of his death:

I am satisfied that the vast majority of the people of Canada are in favour of the continuance and perpetuation of the connection between the Dominion and the mother country. There is nothing to gain and everything to lose by separation. I believe that if any party or person were to announce or declare such a thing, whether by annexation with the neighbouring country, the great republic to the south of us, or by declaring for independence, I believe that the people of Canada would say 'No.' We are content, we are prosperous, we have prospered under the flag of England; and I say that it would be unwise, that we should be lunatics, to change the certain present happiness for the uncertain chances of the future. I always remember, when this occurs to me, the Italian epitaph: 'I was well, I would be better, and here I am.' We are well, we know, all are well, and I am satisfied that the majority of the people of Canada are of the same opinion which I now venture to express here.... I say that it would {181} bring ruin and misfortune, any separation from the United Kingdom. I believe that is the feeling of the present Parliament of Canada, and I am certain that any party, or the supposed party, making an appeal to the people of Canada, or any persons attempting to form a party on the principle of separation from England, no matter whether they should propose to walk alone, or join another country, I believe that the people of Canada would rise almost to a man and say, 'No, we will do as our fathers have done. We are content, and our children are content, to live under the flag of Great Britain.'[7]

Macdonald did not believe in forcing the pace. He looked for a preferential trade arrangement with the United Kingdom, and the establishment of a common system of defence. In all other respects he desired the maintenance of the *status quo*, being content to leave the rest to the future. So much for the Imperial relations. That in all matters relating to its internal affairs Canada should continue to possess the fullest rights of self-government, including exclusive powers of {182} taxation, he considered as an indispensable condition to its well-being.

Nearly twenty-three years have passed since Sir John Macdonald died, and to-day his figure looms even larger in the public mind than on that never-to-be-forgotten June evening when the tolling bells announced to the people of Ottawa the passing of his great spirit. When one takes into account all that he had to contend against — poverty, indifferent health, the specific weakness to which I have alluded, the virulence of opponents, the faint-heartedness of friends — and reflects upon what he accomplished, one asks what was the secret of his marvellous success? The answer must be that it was 'in the large composition of the man'; in his boundless courage, patience, perseverance; and, above all, in his wonderful knowledge of human nature — his power of entering into the hearts and minds of those about him and of binding them to his service. His life is a great example and incentive to young Canadians. Sir John Macdonald began the world at fifteen, with but a grammar-school education; and, possessing neither means nor influence of any kind, rose by his own exertions to a high place {183} on the roll of British statesmen; laboured to build up, under the flag of England, a nation on this continent; and died full of years and honours, amid the nation's tears.

> Looking o'er the noblest of our time,
> Who climbed those heights it takes an age to climb,
> I marked not one revealing to mankind
> A sweeter nature or a stronger mind.

[1] It was commonly understood at this time that Sir Charles Tupper, whose name would naturally first occur in this connection, preferred to remain in England as high commissioner, and, consequently, was not in the running.

[2] Letter to *The Times*, September 1, 1886.

[3] *Weekly Sun*, April 17, 1907.

[4] *Problems of Greater Britain*, p. 44.

[5] 'Some few fools at Montreal are talking about Independence, which is another name for Annexation. The latter cry, however, is unpopular from its disloyalty, and the Annexationists have changed their note and speak of the Dominion being changed into an independent but friendly kingdom. This is simply nonsense. British America must belong either to the American or British System of Government' (Sir John Macdonald to the Hon. R. W. W. Carrall, dated Ottawa, September 29, 1860).

'A cardinal point in our policy is connection with England. I have no patience with those men who talk as if the time must come when we must separate from England. I see no necessity for it. I see no necessity for such a culmination, and the discussion or the mention of it and the suggestion of it to the people can only be mischievous' (*Liberal-Conservative Hand Book*, 1876, pp. 22-3).

'As to Independence — to talk of Independence is — to use Mr Disraeli's happy phrase — "veiled treason." It is Annexation in disguise, and I am certain that if we were severed from England, and were now standing alone with our four millions of people, the consequence would be that before five years we should be absorbed into the United States' (*ibid.*, p. 24).

'The solid substantial advantage of being able to obtain money on better terms than we could on our own credit alone is not the only benefit this guarantee will confer upon us; for it will put a finish to the hopes of all dreamers or speculators who desire or believe in the alienation and separation of the colonies from the mother country. That is a more incalculable benefit than the mere advantage of England's guarantee of our financial stability, great and important as that is' (Debates, House of Commons, 1872, p. 339).

'Gentlemen, we want no independence in this country, except the independence we have at this moment' (*Report of the Demonstration in Honour of the Fortieth Anniversary of Sir John A. Macdonald's Entrance into Public Life*. Toronto, 1885, p. 103).

'Those who disliked the colonial connection spoke of it as a chain, but it was a golden chain, and he for one, was glad to wear the fetters' (Debates, House of Commons, 1875, p. 981).

[6] Montreal *Gazette*, October 25, 1897.

[7] Pope's *Memoirs of Sir John Macdonald*, vol. ii, pp. 220-1.

{184}

BIBLIOGRAPHICAL NOTE

The following works, dealing in whole or in part with the day of Sir John Macdonald, may be consulted: Sir Joseph Pope's *Memoirs of the Right Honourable Sir John Alexander Macdonald* (two vols.: London, Edward Arnold, 1894); Sir John Willison's *Sir Wilfrid Laurier and the Liberal Party* (two vols.: Toronto, Morang, 1903); George R. Parkin's *John A. Macdonald* (Toronto, Morang, 1908); Dent's *The Last Forty Years, or Canada since the Union of 1841* (Toronto, 1881); Castell Hopkins's *Life and Work of Sir John Thompson* (Toronto, 1895); Sir Richard Cartwright's *Reminiscences* (Toronto, Briggs, 1913); Sir Joseph Pope's pamphlet, *Sir John Macdonald Vindicated* (Toronto, 1913); Buckingham and Ross, *The Honourable Alexander Mackenzie: His Life and Times* (Toronto, 1892); Lewis's *George Brown* (Toronto, Morang, 1906); Sir Charles Tupper's *Recollections of Sixty Years in Canada* (London, Cassell, 1914).

Consult also the writings of W. L. Grant, J. L. Morison, Edward Kylie, George M. Wrong, John Lewis, Sir Joseph Pope, and O. D. Skelton in *Canada and its Provinces*, vols. v, vi, and ix.

{185}

For biographical sketches of Robert Baldwin, George Brown, Sir Alexander Campbell, Sir George Cartier, Sir Antoine Dorion, Sir Alexander Galt, Sir Francis Hincks, Sir Louis LaFontaine, John Sandfield Macdonald, Sir Allan MacNab, Sir E. P. Taché, Sir John Rose, and other prominent persons connected with this narrative, see Taylor, *Portraits of British Americans* (Montreal, 1865-67); Dent, *The Canadian Portrait Gallery* (Toronto, 1880); and *The Dictionary of National Biography* (London, 1903).

{187}

INDEX

Seigneurial Tenure and Clergy Reserves Bills, 45 and note; leader of the Clear Grits, 47; his policy of Rep. by Pop., 54-5, 67, 69, 72; his Short Administration in 1858 and humiliation, 57-8, 59; his opinion of the Double Shuffle, 61; joins hands with Macdonald and Cartier to carry through the scheme of Confederation, 42, 71-3, 83; joins the Taché-Macdonald Cabinet, 73, 104; quarrels with his colleagues and resumes his ferocious attacks on the Government, 75 and note; out of Parliament, 95; his letter soliciting campaign funds, 101 n.; his assassination, 18, 118.

Landry, P., speaker of the Senate, 132-3.

Langevin, Sir Hector, a colleague of Sir John Macdonald, 64, 115, 132-3, 140-3.

Laurier, Wilfrid, enters Parliament, 103; Liberal leader, 137; his personality, 160-1.

Liberal party, the, its opposition to the building of the C.P.R., 93, 97 n., 98-9, 100, 118, 119-21 and note; its strength in 1872, 96-7, 102; and the Riel resolution, 132-133; its organized obstruction to Macdonald's Franchise Bill, 136-7; its policy of unrestricted reciprocity with United States, 172. See Baldwin Reformers and Clear Grits.

Liberal-Conservative party, beginning of, 36-9, 40; its programme, 28.

Lower Canada, its development between 1851 and 1861, 47-8; and Rep. by Pop. and Non-sectarian Schools, 54, 56.

M'Carthy, Dalton, his fatuous course in 1887, 158.

Macdonald, Sir John, his birth and parentage, 1, 12-13; boyhood and schooldays, 3-6; called to the bar and opens a law-office in Kingston, 6-7, 14; 'Hit him, John,' 8-9; shoulders a musket in 1837, 9, 15, 16; acts as counsel in the Von Shoultz affair, 9-12, 13; elected to the city council of Kingston, 14; his politics, 16 and note, 22; elected to Assembly, 17; enters Draper's Cabinet, 19 and note; favours Kingston as the seat of government, 26; refuses to sign the Annexation manifesto and advocates the formation of the British America League, 27-8; his policy tending to ameliorate the racial and religious differences existing between Upper and Lower Canada, 31-2 and note, 33-5; attorney-general, 36, 38, 39, 107; his connection with Cartier, 41, 44-5, 47, 78; and Sir Allan MacNab, 41, 43-4; his relations with Brown, 33, 46-7, 58 n., 71, 72-3, 104; prime minister, 54; opposes non-sectarian schools, 55-6; the 'Double Shuffle' episode, 59-62; and Sir John Rose, 64-5; defeated on his Militia Bill, 68-9, 75; his work on behalf of Confederation, 42, 71, 72-3, 74, 75, 99, 100; forms the first Dominion Administration and is created K.C.B., 76-7; and Sir Charles Tupper, 79, 156-8; and Joseph Howe, 79-80, and D'Arcy M'Gee, 81; on Galt, 83; on Galt and Cartwright's defection, 84-5, 86-

7, 166; on his appointment of Hincks as finance minister, 83-4, 85-6; his troubles over the transfer of the North-West, 87-8; and Donald A. Smith, 89-90, 170; member of the Joint High Commission which resulted in the Treaty of Washington, 91-2; his troubles on the eve of the elections of 1872, 93-4, 100; his account of the contests in Ontario, 95-6; the Pacific Scandal, 97-101; and Edward Blake, 109; his National Policy, 112-14, 117; his opinion of Lord Dufferin, 115-116; his relations with the Duke of Argyll, 116-17; his great work in connection with the building of the C.P.R., 50-2, 118-26, 139; the trial and execution of Louis Riel, and the political effect, 127-133; his experience of the fickleness of public opinion, 130-1; his political strategy, 132-3; his desire for a uniform franchise system, 133-4; and the necessity of a property qualification for the right to vote, 134-5; his Franchise Act, 135-8, 139; a believer in the extension of the franchise to single women, 138; on his relations with Langevin, Caron, and Chapleau, 140-3; and his difficulty about his successor, 141; and Sir John Thompson, 146-9; and Sir Alexander Campbell, and Sir Oliver Mowat, 7-8, 149-51; mourns J. H. Pope's loss, 151-2; his reply to Sir C. H. Tupper, 153; against Irish Home Rule, 154-5; on Goldwin Smith, 154-6; on Sir Wilfrid Laurier, 161; an amusing interlude with Honoré Mercier, 162-4; a pointed allusion to his supposed convivial habits, 165-6; on Alonzo Wright, the 'King,' 167; opposed to unrestricted reciprocity with United States, 172; his famous manifesto of 1891, 173-4; and Cecil Rhodes, 174-5; his resemblance to Lord Beaconsfield, 175-6; his Imperialism, 17, 92, 154-5, 174, 176-82; his character, 12-13, 139-40, 158-159, 178-9, 182-3; his death, 182.

Macdonald, John Sandfield, a 'political Ishmaelite,' 63; in power with L. V. Sicotte, 69-70, 81; opposed to Confederation, 74; prime minister of Ontario, 93, 95.

M'Dougall, William, a colleague of Sir John Macdonald, 63; his work on behalf of Confederation, 73, 77; lieutenant-governor of the North-West, 88, 89.

M'Gee, Thomas D'Arcy, a colleague of Sir John Macdonald, 63, 81; his career and assassination, 81-2.

Mackenzie, Alexander, leader of Liberals, 96, 114, 117, 120-121; prime minister, 103, 105; his career and character, 103-104, 133.

Nova Scotia, and Confederation, 73, 79, 93; ratifies Macdonald's policy in connection with the Treaty of Washington, 92, 96.

Ontario, its population and condition in 1815, 2, 3.

Ottawa, chosen as the capital city of Canada, 26 and note, 53, 57.

Pacific Scandal episode, the, 97-101.

Papineau, L. J., leader of the Rouges, 29.

Parliament, and the Rebellion Losses Bill, 20-6, 28; the selection of the capital, 53, 57; the Double Shuffle, 59-62; Conservatives defeated on Militia Bill, 68-9; the double majority principle laid down, 70; Liberals defeated on the National Policy, 113-15, 117; the building of the C.P.R., 119-21, 122, 125 and note; the Electoral Franchise Act, 135-8; a moderating influence begins to be felt, 161.

Pope, J. H., a colleague of Sir John Macdonald, 72, 115, 118; his political sagacity, 151-2.

Prince Edward Island, and Confederation, 73, 74, 96.

Quebec, as a seat of government, 26, 27 n., 52; its population in 1861, 48; Confederation conference in, 74; effect of Riel's execution on, 130-2, 159; and the Jesuits' Estates Act, 162-3.

Radicals of Upper Canada. See Clear Grits.

Rebellion Losses Act, the troubles and disturbances in connection with, 21-6.

Red River insurrection, the, 89, 90.

Rhodes, Cecil, his letter to Sir John Macdonald, 174-5.

Riel, Louis, leader of the Red River insurrection, 89, 93; and the North-West Rebellion, 126-7, 129-30; his trial and execution, 128-9; and its political effect, 130-3, 159.

Rose, Sir John, a colleague of Sir John Macdonald: subscribes to Annexation manifesto, 27; a close friend of Edward VII, 64-5, 67, 68; finance minister, 83; takes up residence in London, 83.

Rose, Lady, the tragic event in her life, 65-7.

Ross, John, a colleague of Sir John Macdonald: joins the MacNab-Morin Cabinet, 37; resigns, 46; and Confederation, 62.

Rouge party, its programme, 29; its alliance with the Clear Grits, 31, 35, 36, 47, 69-70; opposed to Confederation, 74.

Russell, Lord John, defends the Rebellion Losses Bill, 25; in the Hudson's Bay Company investigation, 49.

Ryerson, Rev. Egerton, superintendent of Schools, 55-6.

St Andrews Society of Montreal, 24.

School question, the, 54, 55.

Scott, Thomas, his murder at Fort Garry, 89, 93, 127.

Seigneurial Tenure, abolition of, 37 and note, 45.

Sherwood, Henry, a colleague of Sir John Macdonald, 19-20.

Sicotte, L. V., leader of French-Canadian wing of Liberal Government, 69-70.

Smith, Donald A. See Strathcona, Lord.

Smith, Frank, a colleague of Sir John Macdonald, 152.

Smith, Goldwin, two examples of his malevolence and wit, 103-4; and Sir John Macdonald's Imperialism, 154-6.

Spence, Thomas, a colleague of Sir John Macdonald, 37.

Stephen, George. See Mount Stephen, Lord.

Strathcona, Lord, his first meeting with Sir John Macdonald, 89-90; his mission to Red River Colony, 91; and the C.P.R., 121, 125; two anecdotes concerning, 170-1.

Sweeny, Robert, the tragedy of, 65-7.

Sydenham, Lord, governor-general, 14, 34.

Printed by T. and A. Constable, Printers to His Majesty
at the Edinburgh University Press

THE CHRONICLES OF CANADA

THIRTY-TWO VOLUMES ILLUSTRATED

Edited by GEORGE M. WRONG and H. H. LANGTON

THE CHRONICLES OF CANADA

PART I
THE FIRST EUROPEAN VISITORS

1. THE DAWN OF CANADIAN HISTORY By Stephen Leacock.
2. THE MARINER OF ST MALO By Stephen Leacock.

PART II
THE RISE OF NEW FRANCE

3. THE FOUNDER OF NEW FRANCE By Charles W. Colby.
4. THE JESUIT MISSIONS By Thomas Guthrie Marquis.
5. THE SEIGNEURS OF OLD CANADA By William Bennett Munro.
6. THE GREAT INTENDANT By Thomas Chapais.
7. THE FIGHTING GOVERNOR By Charles W. Colby.

PART III
THE ENGLISH INVASION

PART IV
THE BEGINNINGS OF BRITISH CANADA

PART V
THE RED MAN IN CANADA

15. THE WAR CHIEF OF THE OTTAWAS By Thomas Guthrie Marquis.

16. THE WAR CHIEF OF THE SIX NATIONS By Louis Aubrey Wood.

17. TECUMSEH: THE LAST GREAT LEADER OF HIS PEOPLE By Ethel T. Raymond.

PART VI
PIONEERS OF THE NORTH AND WEST

PART VII
THE STRUGGLE FOR POLITICAL FREEDOM

PART VIII
THE GROWTH OF NATIONALITY

PART IX
NATIONAL HIGHWAYS

31. ALL AFLOAT By William Wood.
32. THE RAILWAY BUILDERS By Oscar D. Skelton.

TORONTO: GLASGOW, BROOK & COMPANY